CAT AMONG THE PIGEONS

A riotous assembly of unrespectable African creatures

David Muirhead

Illustrations by Patricia de Villiers

POWERS SQUARED

Orono, Maine

Text Copyright © David Muirhead, 2020.

Illustration Copyright © Patricia de Villiers, 2020.

All rights reserved.

No part of this book may be used or reproduced
in any manner whatsoever without written consent
from the publisher, except for brief quotations for reviews.
For further information, write Powers Squared, an imprint of Catalyst Press,
email info@catalystpress.org

In North America, this book is distributed by
Consortium Book Sales & Distribution, a division of Ingram.
Phone: 612/746-2600
cbsdinfo@ingramcontent.com
www.cbsd.com

FIRST EDITION
10 9 8 7 6 5 4 3 2 1

Library of Congress Control Number: 2019951216

Originally published by Struik Nature
(an imprint of Penguin Random House South Africa (Pty) Ltd)
Reg. No. 1953/000441/07
The Estuaries No. 4, Oxbow Crescent (off Century Avenue),
Century City, 7441 South Africa
PO Box 1144, Cape Town, 8000 South Africa

Dedicated to

Charlotte Schuster,

my granddaughter,

and all creatures

big and small

ABOUT THE COVER

If you thought you'd picked up a novel by Agatha Christie, you're probably browsing in the wrong section. This is not a murder mystery, although many of the characters in the following pages are adept at killing, deception and detection. Mrs. Christie's book, on the other hand, despite sharing the same title, has nothing to do with cats or pigeons; so if you are in fact interested in wild creatures, rather than murderers, perhaps you're in the right section after all.

"Animals are not brethren, they are not underlings;
they are other nations, caught with ourselves in
the net of life and time."

– Henry Beston

CONTENTS

Foreword vii
Preface xi
Killer Whale 1
Springbok 5
Waterbuck 8
Firefly...11
Elephant 13
Bat-eared Fox 17
Banded Mongoose 20
Tree Squirrel.................................23
African Penguin 26
Wild Dog 29
Hadeda 32
Python 35
Vlei Rat 38
Cockroach 40
Springhare 43
Caracal 46
Cuckoo 49
Vervet Monkey 52
Rhino 55
Albatross 58
Marabou Stork 61
African Buffalo 64
Leopard 68
Lammergeier 71
Golden Orb-Web Spider 74
Pangolin 77
Nightjar 80
Brown Hyena 83
Coelacanth 86
Gorilla 89
Gemsbok 92
Hedgehog 95
Wasp 98
Wildebeest 101
Gecko 104
Rain Frog 107

Aardvark......................................110
Honeybee 113
Octopus 116
Dassie 119
Honey Badger 122
Hippo 125
Klipspringer 128
Spotted Hyena 131
Secretarybird 134
African Clawless Otter 137
Warthog 140
Eland 143
Crow 145
Dugong 148
Boomslang 151
Guineafowl 153
Barn Owl.....................................156
Crocodile 159
Mole-rat.......................................162
White Pelican 165
Baboon 168
Porcupine 171
Egyptian Goose 174
Zebra 177
Cheetah 180
Ground-hornbill 182
Dung Beetle 185
Leatherback Turtle...................188
Bat 191
Bushbaby 194
Chameleon 197
Monitor Lizard...........................200
Giraffe 203
Flamingo 206
Fish Eagle 209
Black-Backed Jackal.................212
Ostrich 215
Fur Seal 218

FOREWORD

by Professor Brian J. Olsen

In 1986, my mother's sister paddled me out to the sandbars of the Long Island Sound with the ostensible purpose of collecting dinner. I marveled at her ability to find any place when rowing while facing the wrong direction. There were cheap plastic buckets involved, and toy shovels that would break given any force greater than a child's bicep. Primary colors. Newly dedicated to the task. And they were stashed alongside woven baskets that had made this trip many, many times, with slats broken, repaired, and broken again. Ash-strip handles that wobbled in their sockets. Once we had cleared away the gulls with our great leaps and kicking of surf—I am sure there was a stated purpose to this mission, but mostly it was dramatic: the flash of white wings against blue and gray, the gulls wheeling and crying in strings ahead of my full sprint, like a telepathic plow of foam lifting into the oncoming tide—there was work to be done.

While I toyed at holes, my aunt wrapped her fingers in tape and dug with her hands, deep and quick after the bubbles and narrow sand openings of hidden creatures. She pulled up razor clams, and cherrystones, and soft shells, and all the while told me their stories. Why they had their names. How they were to be cooked and cleaned. Which ones were best raw and fresh. Or fried, or breaded, or pickled. Which people said which shellfish had other qualities when eaten, but she didn't abide by that. And look! The hole here? Made by a drill snail, rasping with its sharp tongue, precise surgeon beating us to our purpose. And the grand reveal, an empty shell, hinge intact. Wonder.

I walked the shores and dunes and marsh and flat of the Sound with her through my adolescence, till my fingers were also taped, till I was able to fill the baskets as quickly, till I could get a razor clam out fast enough that its defensive squirt of water could be aimed playfully at her face. She still had a new story for each outing. Another reason to pay attention. Another reinvention of the same experience. Stories for the horseshoe crab, the spider crab, the boat shell and jingle shell, the nautilus. Endless wonder.

Our minds are experts at averaging. At filtering out. At focusing on personal motives at the expense of the background. We even call it the background when it's in front of us. It helps us focus, helps us build ourselves, prevents distraction. But it comes at a cost to wonder. And wonder, wonder is the stuff of stories, it is the stuff of surprise and unexpected respect and disbelief made belief. And this is where we gain so much from the body naturalis historia, the layered stories and characters and Kiplinged critters that pull background to foreground and reintroduce us to new family members.

We are in the age of the second, great, human-led extinction. The first came as we spread across the globe. The wooly rhino, the elephant bird, the giant wombat, the mammoth and mastodon, ground sloths and armadillos, the great North American camels and Eurasian Hippopotamuses. The climate changed, we pressed our advantage, and stories fell. Yet Africa kept her secrets. Knew us from before we knew ourselves. Knew us and worked around us. Preserved her wonder, and we kept her stories. But the climate is changing again. And we still press the advantage.

I work in the wildlife department at a small university. We used to train the enforcers and authors of hunting laws. The students came to us because they spent the best hours of their childhood in the bush, and they wanted to make a career of it. They wanted to make sure they could harvest what their grandparents harvested. But those grandparents are disappearing, those students are disappearing, and those harvests are gone. So now we are in the conservation business. Now, the students come to us because they heard about the springbok and the aardvark and the dugong. Now they come for animals they've never even seen before. They were amazed by them, and they come because of the stories. It took me a while to realize that I had come for the same reasons. That I had come because of the surprise skills of a razor clam. The deeper pleasure in knowing hard from soft shell. Knowing when the lobsters molt and how you bait them. The hidden narrative. It was the deeper layers of the created things, the creatura, that I had walked by a thousand times before I was introduced to them again, but for real this time, and they drove my hunger to understand more and protect the processes that made them.

I had another aunt, a great aunt, who was dismissed by my mother.

No heart, she said. Cold inside. "This one time," my mother told me, "you were playing at the top of the stairs, when you were only old enough to be barely walking, and you fell. All the way to the bottom. It was terrifying. Arms and legs rolling. The noise alone was enough to make the house go silent, and then make everyone run toward you with fear. But your Aunt, she was there already. Seated. At her desk at the bottom of the stairs writing something or other. And she didn't. Even. Stand. Up. She just watched the rest of us come to you." And I could picture the inner grinding of her stone heart.

Years later, my mother's sister told me another story. She told me how my great aunt had been visiting us that day during a rare respite from decades of work in an orphanage in the Côte d'Ivoire. That a tumble down a few steps, from a kid who was clearly well enough to cry and stand up and ask for help, was probably something best left to parents. And again, my aunt's story opened my heart to a beautiful being I had never considered family. Because without the story, my great aunt was just my grandfather's sister, with gray hair and a high-buttoned shirt and words I didn't understand, spoken strangely. The background.

My aunt's stories always shifted my perception. Brought background to foreground. Sharpened the wonder and importance that had always been there, just blurred. Her stories gave me new family—either a great aunt who had been cut out, or the animals I still visit, appreciating their lives and the woman who let me look into them for the first time. She was the first person who made me understand that family can be found in unlikely places, in unlikely species, but all of these deeper familial connections provide wonder, and comfort. But emptiness when we lose them. And it's story that weaves these connections, pushing past the easy dismissal, the average apathy, and teaching us the relaxed joy of a long-shared history. Before her stories, there was a time I never thought I would consider my great aunt as family. And a time I would never consider a horseshoe crab as kin.

It's time for us to learn more stories. To open our eyes and be introduced to our family for the first time. To laugh with our vertebrate cousins and deride our mammalian uncle about that thing he knows he does. Wonder is the best child of science and storytelling, and it makes us realize what we have and what we stand to lose. So, repeat these stories and tell them to your nieces and nephews. Don't let a more powerful narrative dissolve these characters into the background until they fade away. Because the razor clam still cracks me up. And I have pretended to shave my beard with it while my son rolled his eyes—eyes that I then immediately squirted with clam juice. Because I knew it could happen. And he didn't. Yet.

Brian J. Olsen, Ph.D.
Associate Professor of Biology & Ecology
Chair of the Department of Wildlife,
*   Fisheries, & Conservation Biology*
Director of the Ecology &
*   Environmental Sciences Program*
University of Maine, Orono, Maine, USA

PREFACE

The first friend millions of little children have, the one they love absolutely, cuddle up to and feel safe with, is usually a bear, a lion, a hippopotamus, a mouse, a giraffe or some other wild creature. Granted, it's made of cloth and stuffed with cotton wool, but it's invariably a recognizable rendition of the real thing. The real thing would, of course, chew the curtains, poop on the carpet, might view the child as a possible menu item, and would certainly do its level best to get out of the nursery, out of suburbia, and back into the wild.

Nevertheless any young child, be they in Boston or Bujumbura, lucky enough to be surrounded by a fluffy menagerie of affable creatures, might well assume that such animals are an integral part of the world they've been born into. And, of course, they'd be right—for the moment.

Until comparatively recently, human beings all around the world regarded wild creatures as fellow travelers on life's winding road, beings with the same right to exist that we assert for ourselves. They played all sorts of lively roles in our tribal mythologies and folklore, a vast body of stories, owing as much to keen observation of animal behavior as to imagination. Eagles and doves helped us communicate with our gods, and a host of other creatures, from the lion to the jackal and the wasp to the frog, taught the fundamentals of wisdom.

In this book I've tried to tap into some of that old empathy. What remains of it is rapidly fading away, as are the futures of all the creatures featured in these pages. To a greater or lesser degree, every one of them is under threat due to habitat loss, poaching and all the other consequences brought about by our burgeoning numbers. The population of Africa has increased sevenfold since I was born, and the picture is repeated in the rest of the world.

It's a different kind of deluge from the one that confronted Noah, but a deluge nevertheless. In that iconic story, common in different forms to many cultures, all the animals are taken on board an ark on the unstated assumption that there couldn't be a new world, at least not one worth living in, without them.

This book is my personal ark of sorts, a way of gathering what I can, though I've been a bit more slapdash than Noah. The creatures that feature in these pages weren't selected according to any kind of divine plan, perhaps not even a moderately sensible plan; they don't appear in the book in alphabetical order, according to species, food preference or any other sort of methodical classification. There are plenty of books about animals that do that but this isn't one of them. What I've tried to do is introduce each creature so that you'll get to know them, not as zoological curiosities but as individuals with lives as rich, in their own way, as our own. Above all, I hope this book will make you chuckle, because laughter, as you know, is a gateway to the heart.

All these creatures live in or around the shores of Africa, though in many cases are not exclusive to the continent. Science tells us that Africa was the cradle of our species, so in a sense this is the familiar old gang, the ones that ate our ancestors, ran away from them, or simply ignored them and got on with the business of living—playing in the sun, seeking shelter from the wind and rain, finding something to eat and drink, courting a mate, and raising young. In other words, doing what we all did then, and what, despite all the dressing up, we still do now.

David Muirhead, *Author*
Vermont, South Africa

KILLER WHALE

Orcus was a monster originally invented by the Etruscans to stoke the fires of Hell. He later emerged as the ogre of fairy tales, fond of eating the flesh of children, among other bad food choices. The slobbering orc in Tolkien's *Lord of the Rings* is probably the most recent manifestation of this archetype.

With all this in mind, "orca" is an odd choice of name to give to a new best friend, but the alternative, "killer whale," seems even more defamatory to their many admirers.

Outside of the ranks of sailors and whalers, little was publicly known about *Orcinus orca* until the mid-1960s, when young orcas began to be captured alive for aquariums. Up until then most folk would probably have gone along with the view expressed by Pliny the Elder, who long ago dismissed them as "mountains of meat with teeth."

When the first captive orcas were installed in tanks and harbor enclosures, the biggest surprise for aquarium directors, apart from the large amounts of money to be made from having one as an attraction, was just how docile and friendly the toothy giants turned out to be. It was even possible to plop scantily-clad young women into the same pond without fear that they would be touched inappropriately, let alone snapped up like canapés. This was precisely the kind of "man-bites-dog" story that appeals to the popular press, and word soon spread. Ticket sales soared and, to meet the burgeoning demand in the 1960s and '70s, more and more orcas, virtually all juveniles, were snatched from the sea.

This sorry episode in the inglorious saga of human-cetacean relations came to an end at about the turn of the century. Audiences and keepers alike began to realize that orcas weren't just titillating monsters but highly intelligent and sensitive creatures, with moods and emotions as complex as ours. Despite their cruel confinement, they behaved far better toward us than we did toward them. Keeping them in swimming pools was a very bad idea.

Public interest helped inspire and fund intensive research, and one of the first major findings was that there were far fewer killer whales in the world's oceans than had been supposed. The population in the Pacific Northwest, which had been the aquariums' principal source of young orcas, amounted to a few hundred at best.

Killer whales are not whales of course, but the largest member of the dolphin family. Despite their being black and white and found all over, we are also now told that there are several different types. Recent research, particularly in the Pacific, has suggested that at least two variants exist: the transients and the residents. Transients seem to wander the seven seas and prey mainly on marine mammals, especially other dolphins, porpoises and whales. Residents, as the name implies, are committed homebodies, stay in the same locale year-round, live in larger family groups or pods, eat mainly fish and never ever take a vacation. The different types seem largely to ignore each other and have even evolved their own dialects of the orca language.

Whatever the cut of their jib or the tone of their voice, killer whales are apex predators, with nothing to fear in the sea. Killers they certainly are, but no more so than a lion or a tiger. The enduring mystery, especially given how we've behaved when we've met them in the wild, is that they haven't taken every available opportunity to chow down on some of us.

It's not as though they've never been exposed to terrestrial food. They've been known to grab seals from pebbly beaches, dislodge penguins and polar bears from ice floes, and even snap up the occasional astonished elk swimming a Canadian river. Flipping a canoe, or even a sizeable yacht, to get at the tidbits with the quivering jelly centers they contain, would be no real challenge. But they've never, barring the occasional aquarium accident, so much as nibbled a single one of us.

A possible answer is that they see us as kindred spirits, or at least as useful idiots. For several decades prior to the demise of the whaling industry, killer whales in the seas off the south coast of New South Wales, Australia, herded humpback whales into a bay near Eden so that whalers could more easily kill them. Their reward was the tongue and the lips, seemingly their favorite cuts. It's difficult to decide who was using whom in this instance, but the relationship went sour when the whalers eventually reneged on the deal and the orcas went off in a huff. Similar stories have arrived from other parts of the world, with the embellishment that orcas occasionally fend off sharks when they try to attack shipwrecked whalers and fishermen.

Putting our conceit aside, in these latter cases (if they happen), it's more likely that the orcas were after the sharks anyway, a favorite prey species. An unspecified number of killer whales recently weighed into the population of great white sharks in South Africa's Walker Bay, much to the consternation of the proprietors of the local shark cage-diving industry. They killed at least three great whites, eating their livers and discarding the rest, proving, if nothing else, that they are choosy about their food, and sometimes wasteful eaters.

They have that in common with most of us and, despite the huge physical disparities, a lot else besides. Other than humans and short-finned pilot whales, orcas are the only known species in which females go through menopause. Various theories have been developed to explain this strange evolutionary quirk, but it seems to be linked in a complex way to longevity, cognition and the importance of familial relationships for survival and success.

Like all dolphins, in addition to their excellent eyesight, killer whales use ultrasound to form a detailed picture of the world under water. Captive orcas, like other dolphins, have purportedly been able to tell when a woman swimming in their tank is pregnant, even if she is in the earliest stages. With such skills, they probably saw through our species long ago. Given their affable attitude toward us, we can only assume that they discovered, in a dark recess, the seed of something worth preserving.

SPRINGBOK

Old Africa knew the springbok by other names, all of which loosely translate as "ray of the sun." The gazelles were especially favored by the sun god who imbued them with magical powers. One happy outcome is that dreaming about a herd of springbok cavorting on the vast, ethereal plains of the Great Karoo yields the dreamer a promise of great wealth.

When it comes to sheer good looks, there's no doubt that the springbok is a crowd-pleaser. If there ever were an event as bizarre as an inter-species beauty contest, many a lass, alas, would run home to her mother in tears. Graceful, slender and long-legged, with a snow-white face, a golden coat and bold side stripes, as well as other more subtle cosmetic touches, these antelope seem to know they were really born for the swanky salons of Paris, London and Milan.

When excited or frightened and sometimes, it seems, just because there's an audience, they repeatedly bounce into the air, 2 meters (6.5 feet) and more, back arched, hooves bunched and legs held stiffly together, as though they're on pogo sticks. As part of this dramatic routine, the flap on their rump inverts into a fan of dazzling white hairs, more than worthy of a headline act at the Moulin Rouge. The whole performance is known as "pronking," derived from an Afrikaans word which, if you ignore the professorial chit chat, means "showing off."

According to one theory, this may be exactly what they're doing. Vanity aside, such displays advertise the buck's fitness and agility. An approaching predator, duly impressed, gets the message and turns its attention to some other unlucky couch potato. If not, the buck can further prove its point by streaking away at up to 88 kilometers (55 miles) per hour.

Perhaps nature knew her design department had hit the bullseye when it came up with the springbok. In earlier times she churned them out by the million. Accounts from awed and trapped rural observers in the 1800s record how galloping masses of springbok, tightly packed mega-herds stretching further than the eye could see, took five days and more to sweep past lonely Karoo farmhouses. Their sharp little hooves left much dust and devastation, including a swathe of corpses belonging to small creatures unable to get out of the way. Casualties among the antelope's own ranks provided additional free meals for the carnivorous camp followers puffing or flapping along behind.

Uncontrolled hunting and the spread of barbed wire put an end to such grand migrations long ago. They still happen on occasion in parts of Botswana and Namibia, albeit as mere shadows of the big events of yesteryear, triggered now, as then, by local droughts and the distant scent of greener pastures.

Springbok are grazers and browsers, nibbling on selected grasses, shrubs and succulents and can obtain virtually all the water they need from plants and morning dew. Depending on local conditions, they seldom, if ever, need to visit a pond or a stream. This was just as well in days gone by because perennial surface water was practically non-existent in their preferred habitat, the huge arid plains of southwestern Africa.

Springbok are relatively prolific breeders, with births tending to cluster around the onset of the rainy season when food is at its most abundant. Females first come into estrus at six to seven months and a single calf, rarely twins, is born five to six months later. In theory, and often in practice if a young calf dies, females are able to produce two offspring in a single year. The calf usually stays with its mother until she gives birth again, something that can occur in as little as six months. When this happens adolescent males are inclined and encouraged to leave and join a bachelor herd.

Males reach breeding age only when they're about two years old. They need a further year to mature and bulk up sufficiently to engage in the potentially injurious or fatal contests necessary to secure a territory. On average, a successful male manages to hold onto his patch for six months to a year, though during that time he repeatedly has to fight off home invasions. He demonstrates his pride in possession by strutting about and ostentatiously urinating and defecating, rear legs akimbo, on the same chosen boundary spots, exactly the kind of thing that would rapidly get you arrested if you tried it on your suburban borders.

The springbok has long held center stage in southern Africa. Many of the Bushmen's stories and mystic customs revolved around them. They were living symbols that all was well with the world, their honey-colored flanks symbolizing good health and abundance; a thinning in their numbers, or their total absence, heralding troubling times for their diminutive hunters.

This emblematic role has continued into modern times. The springbok is South Africa's national animal and the totem of the country's rugby team, whose members are not above a little imitative pronking themselves, notably in the lineouts. Although now mainly confined to game farms, their numbers remain buoyant. In that we can take comfort. According to old tribal lore, the death of the last springbok will be a day of doom for all the peoples of southern Africa.

WATERBUCK

It might cost you in lost party invitations, but having a reputation for smelling and tasting disgusting is a major advantage if you want to stay alive in the bush. Even if there's a big white target painted on your rear end, no problem: a charging lion will likely pull up short and mutter that it mistook you for something less revolting.

Despite taking regular baths, waterbuck are famous for having a personal hygiene problem so ferocious that other animals stay a million miles upwind. That's a bit unfair, of course, not to mention a wild distortion, but not wholly devoid of truth. They do indeed have a strong, musky smell, somewhere between turpentine and a pair of socks on Stage 10 of the Tour de France. Even when they've pedaled away, you can still pick up the odor in the places they've been.

The source of this stink is an oily secretion exuded from glands in the skin. Its purpose is not completely understood but there's strong evidence that it acts, among other things, as an insect repellent. Tsetse flies, to name but one insufferable bug, stay well clear of waterbuck. This has not gone unnoticed by cattle farmers in Kenya. As an experiment, they tried replicating Eau de Waterbuck and hanging the concoction in dispensers around the necks of their cows; tsetse fly bites reduced by up to 90 percent.

Bugs are one thing, but nature never hands out totally free passes; the notion that waterbuck don't get attacked and eaten by lions and crocodiles is a myth. When the menu is being passed around out on the veld, lions might rest their eyes a little longer on the zebra kebabs and buffalo steaks but they will opt for waterbuck cutlets now and again. Crocodiles gave up being picky millions of years ago; if you live in a pond that 20 hippopotamuses use as a toilet, it doesn't seem to matter.

Odoriferous issues aside, waterbuck seem to be on the wrong continent. A thick gray coat with a shaggy ruff around the neck seems more appropriate for Aspen, Colorado or Chamonix, France than tropical Africa. Perhaps that's why they usually hang around rivers and streams where they can enjoy the cooling waters and the welcoming shade of riverside trees. But the thick, hollow hair around their necks does have a sensible purpose: according to one theory, it provides buoyancy when they go swimming, helping to keep their heads above water.

The common waterbuck's most distinctive fashion feature is, of course, the white ring on its backside, the subject of tired jokes about wet paint and toilet seats. This is smudged on the rear end of the defassa waterbuck, into more of a patch than a circle. Where their ranges overlap, the two animals interbreed and are essentially the same species, so variations inevitably arise. In southern Africa, the common waterbuck is prevalent, and the posterior markings are usually at their most distinctive. The antelope were revered by some southern tribes, at least in part because the circle of white hairs was thought to symbolize the genitalia of the Great Earth Mother.

Despite the name, waterbuck are not so obsessed with aquatic pursuits that they spend the entire day, or even much of it, splashing about. But they do need to drink every day, so when the time comes to settle down, first choice is a river or lake-front property. It's also good to have somewhere safe to plunge into in case a lion with a peg on its nose happens to come galloping over the hill.

Territories are not marked out in the way favored by so many other animals, namely defecating and urinating on the boundary; not to belabor the point, but that's hardly necessary, in the circumstances. Once established, a male waterbuck takes his property rights very seriously and a good part of every day is spent in facing off with the neighbors. The trick is to stand

erect and sublime at such times, looking official and important. Point made, both neighbors then back off and go to lunch. Visiting bachelors are tolerated, providing they're obsequious; only when a young buck pitches up with a determined look on his face, obviously intent on getting into the property market, come what may, is it necessary to resort to violence.

Female waterbuck, in loose herds and accompanied by their young, range over a number of male territories, lingering here and there as the mood takes them, but coyly refusing to be pinned down on a permanent basis.

When it's time for an expectant mother to give birth she leaves the herd to find a secluded spot in thick vegetation. Soon after the birth she leaves her newborn calf to its own devices, wandering up to a kilometer (six-tenths of a mile) away during the day and only returning to suckle two or three times between dusk and dawn. Each time, she thoroughly cleans her calf before leaving, endeavoring to remove as much scent as possible. Nevertheless, no doubt conscious of the fatal attraction of Mom's own overblown perfume, junior takes the precaution of changing hiding places after each visit. Sadly, these precautions don't always work, and a high proportion of newborns fall prey to leopards and hyenas. The calf's largely solitary and very scary daytime existence ends after about four to five weeks, when it is finally able to join its mother and the dubious safety of a changeable herd.

The Batswana name for the waterbuck is *serwalabotloko* which, loosely translated, means "the one who carries away pain." The poetry derives from an ancient custom. When a tribal chief was ailing, and all other traditional treatments had failed, a male waterbuck was captured, trussed up and carried into the old man's hut. Great care was taken to ensure that the animal was not hurt or injured in any way. The chief would be raised from his bed so that he could grasp the animal's horns, and fervently pray to be cured. The buck was then carried back to where it had been found, and released. If it ran into the bush, the chief would die; if it chose to plunge into water, he would recover.

Perhaps, in a strange way, being the butt of ribald jokes has helped ensure that the waterbuck continues the mystic mission ascribed to it in African tradition; laughter is, after all, one of nature's most powerful antidotes for pain.

FIREFLY

If you'd been paying proper attention in chemistry class you'd know that adenosine triphosphate (ATP to its friends) is a critically important macro molecule that acts as a power broker for virtually every cell in your body. All living creatures depend on it to do the things they do.

The forebears of fireflies worked out long ago that when you combine ATP with oxygen, calcium and the chemical luciferin in the presence of an enzyme called luciferase, light is produced. It's tempting to speculate that if our own ancient ancestors had done their science homework properly, our noses would also light up when required and we wouldn't need to burn billions of tons of fossil fuels to power our bedside reading lamps.

Firefly is a colloquial name for over 2,000 species of bioluminescent insects that live in the world's tropical and temperate zones. With the exception of a cave-dwelling fungus gnat that lives in New Zealand and Australia and generally minds its own business, none are flies and none can set the world on fire. Unlike even our most energy efficient bulbs, the light they produce generates virtually no heat.

True fireflies are nocturnal beetles, members of the *Lampyridae* family. They favor moist conditions and are hence usually found in or near marshes or where there's plenty of damp leaf litter about, typically in forested or wooded areas by rivers, ponds and lakes. In their larval phase some are semi-aquatic.

Already boffins in chemistry, fireflies of the *Photuris* genus have gone to the top of the class in physics too, refining and sculpting the edges of the translucent scales in their exoskeleton to optimize light output. This neat trick has been experimentally copied to make LED lights 50 percent more efficient.

Not only adult beetles light up. The larvae and even the eggs of many species also emit an eerie glow. The supposition is that the bugs first evolved their light show as a means of warning predators not to eat them. When alarmed, they exude a substance that tastes disgusting and is toxic to many undiscerning consumers. In the lethal trial-and-error process nature favors, luminosity was a clever way of getting that message across.

But having mastered the science, fireflies subsequently worked out that flashing off and on is also a nifty way to communicate with each other, particularly when it's time to find a mate. Some reprobates have gone one step further. They imitate the amorous flashes of other related species to lure unsuspecting suitors to join them for lunch.

Because there are so many different species, each adopting a slightly different approach to life's chores and conundrums, it's not surprising that we're a bit confused about who's who in the firefly zoo. About 30 species live in southern Africa, varying in size from 5 to 30 millimeters (0.2 to 1.2 inch). Unsurprisingly, the name firefly is usually ascribed to those that fly, flitting about and flicking their little lamps on and off as the mood takes them. In some species only the male has wings and very large eyes but doesn't light up at all; the female is flightless and emits a steady glow when ready to attract a mate. Females of this species look as though they never quite made it out of the larval stage and are hence often known as glow-worms. In the world at large, glowworm is a name happily bandied about without any particular reference to entomological exactitude.

The bulk of a firefly's modest lifespan is spent in the larval stage. They potter about in the underbrush and even underground, hunting and eating snails and worms. When they become adults most of them don't eat at all, though some species find time in their busy schedule to take the occasional sip of nectar. Such brief visits to the juice bar aside, adult life for a firefly is firmly focused on finding a mate and, when conditions are favorable, their large numbers can produce an awe-inspiring light show.

Inexplicable things that shine in the night tend to ignite the human imagination and fireflies predictably attract more than their fair share of superstition. A legend of the Ewe people, who live in Togo and Ghana, holds that vampires routinely take the form of fireflies. If you're stupid enough to catch one and put it in a jar, it will promptly overcome that inconvenience by assuming its true form and then eat your liver. In stark contrast, Japanese poets have long evoked the firefly as a symbol of enduring love and hope. In other cultures they are believed to provide some sort of electrical utility for elves and fairies. If this is indeed the case, we can sympathize with these diminutive citizens of the netherworld as they no doubt register regular complaints about the erratic nature of this essential public service.

ELEPHANT

African and Asian elephants have only once fought against each other in a formal battle. The result was a pushover for the Asians. The encounter occurred during the Battle of Gaza in 217 BC between the forces of the Egyptian pharaoh, Ptolemy IV, and Antiochus III of the Seleucid kingdom.

To be fair, Antiochus had 102 Asian elephants in his army, whereas Ptolemy could muster only 73 reluctant Africans, rounded up on the savannas of Eritrea. They were smaller than their Asian counterparts, from a subspecies now extinct. They took one look at the trumpeting horde of Oriental pachyderms, ditched their keepers, and promptly stampeded off the battlefield. Despite this disappointing performance, Ptolemy's army still somehow managed to win the day.

While it's certainly nothing to brag about, trained elephants have been used in wars for over 3,000 years. Virtually all these combatants were from Asia, but the elephants that famously plodded over the snowy Alps with Hannibal to attack the Romans on their home turf were almost certainly African. They were probably sourced from the slopes of the Atlas Mountains in Morocco, and may, once again, have been of a slightly smaller subspecies now no longer with us.

The big tuskers that roamed the forests and savannas south of the vast Sahara were inaccessible to the warmongers of the old world, so they couldn't easily be recruited to join the ongoing carnage. By the time this changed, high explosives had been invented and their services on the battlefield were no longer required.

An elephant's main preoccupation in life is eating rather than fighting. To meet the nutritional requirements of their huge bodies they need to consume about 170 kilograms (375 pounds) of vegetation every day, which can mean munching for up to 18 hours in every 24. Their digestive systems are also not wildly efficient, so a significant proportion of what goes in one end comes out the other, only partly the worse for wear. That's good news for dung beetles, of course, and all the other creatures that make a living in the recycling business; but it does mean that any "all you can eat" restaurants would quickly flip their signs and lock the doors if they saw a boisterous party of elephants coming down the street toward them.

As you'd expect from big eaters, elephants tuck away a wide variety of plant matter, including grass, leaves, bark, twigs, seed pods and fruits. They routinely break branches or push over entire trees, some quite sizeable, to get at what they want. In the natural scheme of things their destructive feeding habits don't matter much, and can even eventually be beneficial for other plant—and even other animal—species. But when large numbers of elephants are artificially confined to an inadequate area the result can be catastrophic for the entire ecosystem, including the elephants themselves.

African elephants used to wander wherever they pleased, north to south and east to west, from the temperate shores of Table Bay to the tropical beaches of East Africa's Great Lakes and beyond. Many of their old migration trails through coastal mountain passes and thick forests were used by Thomas Bain and other road and railway engineers as they opened up the hinterlands of Africa. Ironically, among the first to make use of these routes were professional hunters, the precursors of a great slaughter that soon decimated the elephant populations, as well as vast numbers of other African creatures on the plains of the great plateaus.

Of course, professional hunters were mainly after elephant tusks, which, if it weren't a commonly accepted fact, would surely be regarded as utterly bizarre. It is the only instance in the history of life on earth in which one species has preyed on another with the express purpose of extracting two of its teeth. An alien visitor might reasonably conclude that we were a species of mad dentists.

Elephant tusks are modified incisors and very useful to the rightful owner in a variety of ways, including as levers, for digging, stripping bark from trees, as well as in defense and offense. They are purely ornamental for anyone else. With the advent of synthetic materials, ivory is no longer even used for billiard balls or piano keys, but nevertheless demand, principally from China, remains insatiable. Buyers, legal or otherwise, are prepared to pay huge sums.

Big-game hunters took a heavy toll on elephants in Africa but they had become rather ridiculous anachronisms by the middle of the 20th century. Their place was taken by men with AK-47s who needed money, mainly to buy more AK-47s. By the 1960s the large-scale wars that the African elephant had once managed to avoid had finally arrived on their home

ground, with truly devastating results for the species.

Elephants are intelligent and emotional animals, and they must surely wonder where it will all end. Those unfortunates charged with the horrible task of culling elephants in overpopulated areas know that it is more humane to kill all the animals in a given family, such is the overwhelming misery and inconsolable distress of any survivors.

Elephants endeavor to support and lift an ailing matriarch or family member, and to hover around a corpse for hours, seemingly undecided about what to do. Even the bleached bones of long-dead elephants garner intense interest; in a strange communion they gently touch the remains, particularly the tusks and the jaws, with the tip of their trunk.

For the time being the behemoths can only soldier on, making the best of the parcels of wild land presently left to them by humanity's burgeoning numbers and relentless warring. But for the largest land animal on earth, there are inevitable stresses and strains in being confined.

When they reach the age of 12 or so, young male elephants are shown the door by the family matriarch and in the normal course of events join up with mature bulls which, like it or not, are responsible for their higher education. In recent years, young bull elephants in Hluhluwe-Imfolozi in KwaZulu-Natal lacked such role models and somewhat unfairly focused their teenage frustrations on rhinos, bowling them about like beach balls. They killed several and the mayhem only subsided with the intervention of two huge mature elephant bulls trucked in from the Kruger National Park.

It is a sad indictment of our own species that we seem incapable of finding such mountains of wisdom and placid authority to bring an end to our own bloody and perpetual squabbles.

BAT-EARED FOX

The bat-eared fox only made it into the exclusive *Canidae* club by a whisker. It mainly eats termites and that's a bit like being a vegetarian at a *Blou Bulle* braai.[1] To add to the confusion, it often sports a black bandit mask, a bit like a racoon. Nevertheless, a fox it is indeed, even if it has been partly named after an aerial rodent.

Nicknaming someone after an anatomical anomaly is frowned upon in polite society, but there's simply no escaping the fact that those whopping ears are the fox's most distinctive feature. The reason they've evolved to look like satellite dishes is that they have a similar function. They don't pick up Digital Satellite TV, which given current content is probably just as well, but they do enable the fox to eavesdrop on subterranean chatter. If you had a pair of ears like that you'd probably be astonished at the kind of racket termites, grubs and larvae make as they go about their daily chores. A dung beetle grub breaking out of its subterranean egg and eagerly looking forward to a lifetime of rolling elephant poop is likely to have a truncated career if a bat-eared fox happens to be in the immediate vicinity.

Another peculiarity that distinguishes bat-eared foxes from other canids is their teeth; proportionally they're a lot smaller but these foxes have more of them—an extra set of molars in both their upper and lower jaws. Coupled with a muscular adaptation in the lower jaw, this enables them to chomp insects at a ferocious rate, easily eclipsing the dental dexterity of a greedy kid who doesn't want to share his packet of jellybeans.

Eschewing such selfish behavior, bat-eared foxes are social and can often be found in groups, amicably sharing popular foraging sites. Such groups usually consist of a mating pair and their offspring but the neighbors occasionally invite themselves over and gatherings of a dozen or more of various ages are not uncommon. In areas where human beings and

---

1 A barbeque for fans of the Blue Bulls rugby team. Similar to a Texas-style barbeque for a football game.

other diurnal predators are regularly out and about the foxes are mainly nocturnal, particularly during the summer months. But in some parts of South Africa, notably the Great Karoo, they often forage during the day in winter, preferring to snuggle up at night when an icy wind blows, just like the rest of us.

Unlike warthogs and other squatters of the African veld, bat-eared foxes usually dig their own dens but they will make use of disused aardvark burrows when they're available. Either way, they keep their options open and usually have two or more dens within their home range, each with several meters (10 feet or more) of tunnels and a couple of relatively capacious chambers.

The diminutive beasts—generally no longer than 50–60 centimeters (1.5-2 feet) excluding the bushy tail, and tipping the scales at a modest 4–5 kilograms (9-11 pounds)—choose to live in arid grasslands, by and large, where the grasses are kept relatively short by ungulates. It is, of course, no coincidence that such habitats are also favored by the termites that form up to 80 percent of their diet. To relieve the monotony, the foxes also prey on a variety of other bugs, including grasshoppers and beetles, as well as lizards and mice and a little bit of carrion, when it's available. Their diet supplies most of their water needs, which is just as well, given that perennial ponds and streams are invariably rare in the places where they choose to live.

Although exceptions have been noted, bat-eared foxes are usually monogamous. The pair produces a litter of up to six pups, which are then wholly dependent on their mother's milk for 3–4 months. Unusually, the male is a stay-at-home dad during this period, guarding, grooming and playing with the cubs and, where necessary, moving them between dens. The female needs to be out and about, gobbling up enough termites and bugs to ensure a regular milk supply. She never returns with tidbits, nor offers up the kind of regurgitated yuck other youngsters sometimes have to put up with—it's milk or starve. The cubs get to sample their first juicy termite only once they've been weaned. During the interludes when she is home, the male seizes the opportunity to dash off to the local termitarium to quickly stuff his face, and woe betide him if he stops off for a pint at the The Wiley Fox on the way home.

Sadly, he may never come home. Given the foxes' largely nocturnal habits and furtive natures, the only one most people are ever likely to see will be dead by the side of the road. A gloomy study by the Endangered Wildlife Trust turned up 38 dead foxes in two days on a road to the Kalahari, which likely included entire families. They sometimes use the convenient roads that crisscross their range to travel about; along the way they discover the bloody remains of some other luckless animal or bird—a seemingly easy meal, which can prove fatal. Although very nimble, relying on their dodging ability and speed to escape other predators, bat-eared foxes can seldom dodge a car coming out of the night at 120 kilometers (75 miles) per hour.

There are two subspecies of *Otocyon megalotis*, one living in East Africa, north to Ethiopia, and the other ranging from Zambia and Angola into southern Africa. Thankfully, for the time being at least, neither is thought to be endangered.

BANDED MONGOOSE

Mungos mungo may sound like the name of a dubious character in a Victorian novel—perhaps the swarthy villain in a lurid and steamy tale set in the African jungle—but it is in fact the scientific name for the banded mongoose. These petite and sociable carnivores are equally adept at playing the villain or the hero in real-life dramas.

In fiction, mongooses are invariably lumbered with the dangerous chore of despatching cobras and other poisonous snakes. Rikki-Tikki-Tavi, the legendary slayer of the slithery and evil husband-and-wife team, Nag and Nagaina, set the exacting standard in Rudyard Kipling's short story of the same name. The tale, endlessly reworked in print and film, firmly coupled mongooses in the popular imagination with the legless reptiles.

Given a choice, the banded mongoose can take them or leave them—preferably the latter, especially if they happen to be butch, black, 3 meters long and have a really bad attitude. In common with others of their species, they do have some immunity to snake venom, at least those containing neurotoxins, but they don't go out of their way to prey on big poisonous snakes, and avoid them when they can. Small harmless ones are no problem, and are no doubt quite delicious, but true nirvana for a banded mongoose is discovering a big pile of elephant dung covered in crunchy beetles. When that happens, the finder positively twitters with excitement, thereby inadvertently attracting the attention of the rest of the foraging clan who quickly hurry over to muscle in on the feast.

Banded mongooses tend to form the largest packs of any of their species, sometimes numbering in excess of 30 individuals of varying ages and sexes, including up to four or five breeding pairs. Hierarchies are organized in terms of age, chutzpah and personal charisma rather than gender, but the leader of the pack is more likely to be a female than a male. Outsiders are not welcome, though nature quietly manages to sneak in eligible young males from time to time to help stir up the gene pool. Smaller rival groups are emphatically chased away, and pitched battles occur when opposing

packs of similar strength are both pumped up with righteous indignation.

Individual courage and pack loyalty is seldom in doubt; when a crisis looms, they've always got each other's backs. Faced with a manageable predator, such as a jackal, they cluster tightly together, crouching, standing, doing push-ups, running on the spot—just about any communal gymnastics to convince the intruder that it is facing something a whole lot bigger, or at least a lot more complicated, than a family of teeny-weeny banded mongooses. If the adversary, such as a leopard or a spotted hyena, is totally out of the mongooses' league, they bolt for the nearest hiding place, of which they usually have several scouted out within their home range. *In extremis*, they head for the nearest tree.

In one documented incident, worthy of the mongoose equivalent of the Victoria Cross, a martial eagle snatched a juvenile banded mongoose and took it to a roost in a nearby tree. The eagle's astonishment must have been something to behold when the alpha male suddenly appeared on the branch, having climbed up the tree to sort him out. Junior apparently turned out fine, barring a few bruises and scratches.

Banded mongooses inhabit large parts of sub-Saharan Africa, from Sudan in the north, in a broad corridor across to The Gambia in the west, and all the way down to South Africa. They avoid true deserts and forested areas, including the Congo Basin, instead favoring lightly wooded savannas, especially where old termite mounds remain. With their multiple entrances and exits, these are easy to adapt for use as communal dens. Aardvark burrows and any other structure, natural or man-made, that gets them out of sight and snugly tucked up for the night, can be pressed into service. On an early morning stroll in Kilolo, a suburb of Kampala in Uganda, I was astonished to see what looked like a huge hairy python rapidly appearing from a roadside storm-water drain. It turned out to be a large pack of banded mongooses, emerging nose to tail in the dawn light from their temporary digs.

When traveling from place to place the pack usually moves in a tight, purposeful column, worming over the intervening terrain until they reach a foraging site. On arrival they spread out, each to his own patch, scratching in the earth, turning over leaf litter, small rocks and pebbles, and all the while keeping an ear cocked in case one of their colleagues has an elephant dung eureka moment. Discovering a bird's egg, a snail, a centipede or an armor-plated beetle calls for special treatment. Because it lacks the dental equipment to crack open such a prize, the mongoose backs up to a convenient rock, bends over, and hurls the item between its rear legs. It usually shatters first time.

When the breeding season rolls around, banded mongooses start giggling—a phenomenon that must be disconcerting for pious onlookers who regard procreation as a serious business. Fun over, the pregnant females in a given pack synchronize their birthing to within two or three days of each other. This is probably to ensure that nobody gets jealous and starts having dark thoughts about infanticide. In consequence, large packs can find themselves looking after litters of upwards of 10 pups and it becomes a communal effort. A lactating female will nurse any pup, not just her own. When it's time for the pack, including the mothers, to go foraging during the day, a responsible adult remains at the den to keep an eye on the valuables.

Banded mongooses are known to take care of their sick and injured, grooming them and helping them gain access to food. This, perhaps more than their much-vaunted prowess in slaying giant serpents, sets them apart as diminutive heroes of the animal kingdom.

TREE SQUIRREL

The Vikings imagined a squirrel inhabiting the branches of Yggdrasil, the World Tree. His name was Ratatoskr, which translates from the Old Norse as "Drill-tooth" and he was a bit of a scallywag. He kept himself busy trying to stir up trouble between an imperious eagle perched at the top of the tree and a cantankerous worm that lived in its roots. Why Ratatoskr was so intent on starting a quarrel between these two polar opposites remains unclear, though he must have had his reasons.

Squirrels are portrayed as busybodies and purveyors of malicious gossip in the folklore of many cultures, a fact probably best explained by their inquisitive and furtive natures. They always seem to want to know exactly what's going on, spying and eavesdropping from a perch on a branch and vanishing as soon as they're spotted. It's easy to imagine that they've scampered off to tattletale about what they've seen or overheard.

The tree squirrel (aka Smith's bush squirrel, *Paraxerus cepapi*) is true to form, living a largely arboreal existence in the savanna woodlands of East and West Africa, extending its range south as far as the northern provinces of South Africa. These squirrels are small rodents, tipping the scales at a modest 200 grams (7 ounces) and reaching a total length of 300 millimeters (12 inches), half of which consists of a bushy tail. The color of their coat varies regionally, tending to pale gray in the west and brown in the east. All have white bellies and notably lack the white side stripes of the ground squirrel.

A much larger foreign cousin, the gray squirrel, is confined to the leafy suburbs of the Cape Peninsula. Native to the hardwood forests of North America, the grays were originally imported to South Africa by Cecil John Rhodes to enliven the branches of the imported oaks and pines on his Groote Schuur Estate. They are more or less stuck in their Cape enclave, dependent on exotic trees for their survival, and thus pose little threat to the local ecology.

Diurnal and essentially vegetarian, tree squirrels live a busy life scampering about in a never-ending and seemingly frantic search for seeds, nuts and berries, though like most rodents they also enjoy the occasional bug. The search frequently takes them down to the ground but they never stray far from a tree and will bolt up the trunk and back into the branches at the slightest hint of danger. Ever alert, they rely on their speed and agility to evade predators, and there are not many creatures capable of catching them unawares. The principal threat is from raptors and snakes.

Some squirrels choose a solitary existence but more often than not they live in small territorial family groups, consisting of a mating pair and their offspring. At night the family shares sleeping quarters, wrapping themselves up in their bushy tails. The bedroom consists of a hole in a tree and explains why the creatures favor species such as ironwood, which routinely provide such accommodation as well as sustenance. The group frequently engages in mutual grooming, thereby sharing a scent, which helps establish family credentials and promotes social cohesion.

A solitary tree squirrel has to live on its wits and the advantage of being part of a family soon becomes obvious when a snake is spotted. Like birds, squirrels mob the slithery intruder. They approach with caution from all sides, working themselves up, flicking their tails to and fro like bushy whips and all the while emitting sharp clicking noises. It's usually enough to send the snake packing but on rare occasions, assuming the serpent is slow on the uptake and doesn't look too big or deadly, they'll mount a physical attack.

Tree squirrels are seasonal breeders in the southern part of their range, mating in August and giving birth to two or three pups in October or early November. The young leave the nest within three weeks to forage on their own, though they continue to suckle for a further two or three weeks. They reach sexual maturity after six months and are then promptly booted out to make their own way in the world.

Northern hemisphere squirrels are famous for preparing winter larders by hoarding caches of seeds and nuts, planting them in holes in the ground and then forgetting where they put them. This habit fortuitously promotes the growth of new trees and probably explains at least in part why oaks and other seed- and nut-bearing trees produce such copious quantities for their industrious but absent-minded distributors.

Although they're not faced with the same extremes of climate, African tree squirrels also indulge in hoarding behavior, taking advantage of seasonal bounty and sensibly preparing for leaner times. Whether they truly forget where they've put their caches is not really known but, in keeping with Ratatoskr's dodgy reputation, they're undoubtedly alert enough to routinely steal from their neighbors' secret stashes.

AFRICAN PENGUIN

"Penguin" was originally a colloquial name for the great auk, a northern hemisphere look-alike that was barely related. Once numbering in the millions, the flightless auks were relentlessly slaughtered over the centuries for their meat and fat. The last pair was killed on the July 3, 1844 by two Icelandic fishermen, commissioned to commit the dastardly deed by a museum. Knowing that the species was in peril, the museum curators had decided—in the interests of science, *nogal*—to get hold of a couple of stuffed ones for their dusty shelves before it was too late.

If the penguins of the southern hemisphere had any inkling of this crass calamity, they would surely have wished that their discoverers had chosen a less ominous name. The African penguin was the first of its kind to be encountered and named by European mariners as they fiddled about in the fickle winds at the Cape of Good Hope in the late 15th century. Fast-forward to the mid 1800s and there was already little doubt that the arrival of men in boats had set the scene for the birds to suffer the same sad fate as the auk.

African penguins chose to live along the temperate shores of southern Africa, understandably leaving their close cousins to enjoy the icy and inhospitable wastes of Antarctica, and other grim southerly addresses. They made a home for themselves on the numerous offshore islands dotting the South African and Namibian coasts. The islands offered safety from most predators and they were all within relatively easy reach of rich fishing grounds.

Even at these relatively benign latitudes it's important to get out of the African sun, particularly when raising a family. A bonus of the islands was that many had accumulated a thick coating of guano, soft enough to excavate a burrow, and absorbent enough to deal with the rain when it fell. If you keep your mind firmly distracted from the origin of this unique encrustation, guano makes a very cozy home.

It also makes a fantastic fertilizer. At almost the same moment as the last pair of great auks were being scientifically dispatched in the northern hemisphere, entrepreneurs discovered the vast deposits of guano in southern Africa—over 20 meters (65 feet) deep on some islands—and set about removing them. When the frenzy was finally over, some 40 years on, the penguins that remained found themselves left with bare rock, their eggs exposed to the gulls and the sun.

Unfortunately, the gulls weren't the only egg collectors. In one of those inexplicable waves that trigger fads and fashions in human populations, penguin eggs became a highly popular item in South African kitchens at the start of the 20th century. Lawrence Green, the peripatetic author, had many fine egg recipes, and was happy to share them with his readers. To be fair, like one of the tearful characters in Lewis Carroll's poem *The Walrus and the Carpenter*, in later life he lamented the seemingly inevitable demise of the parent birds.

About 2 million African penguins are estimated to have existed at the start of the 20th century; today there are fewer than two hundred thousand, and the numbers are still dropping. Their chronically reduced ranks make them ever more vulnerable as a species to both natural and man-made threats—and the latter keep remorselessly piling up. Aging and rusty ships rounding the Cape routinely leak oil from their bunkers, and occasionally come apart altogether, dumping their entire noxious cargo into the sea; overfishing has led to a drastic reduction in fish stocks; and plastic and

other pollutants in the sea set all kinds of lethal traps.

African penguins were once in a prime position to send gloating postcards back to their relatives in the snowy wastes of Antarctica, bragging about the sunshine and the good life, but they must surely now be consumed by doubts. If so, they show no sign of it. Smartly attired and as determined as ever, it's business as usual for the plucky survivors.

Penguins hunt by sight and each busy day begins bright and early, especially if there are chicks to be fed. Comically clumsy on land, in the sea penguins are more aqua dynamic than the most bragged-about submarine, and infinitely more maneuverable. They travel to fishing grounds in hunting parties of up to 60 birds, swimming 3 meters (10 feet) below the surface, on average, and popping up every 20 seconds or so to take a breath. A daily round trip can involve distances of 30 to 40 kilometers (20-25 miles), and much longer than that if fish are hard to find.

It's an arduous commute by any standards, not made any easier by the thugs lining the route. The deadbeats who threaten late-night travelers in the dark recesses of the London or New York underground are purring pussy cats compared with the seals, sharks and orcas that make it their sharp-toothed business to waylay commuting penguins.

Given this history and their apparent stoicism in the face of epic human greed, it is not surprising that the inoffensive little birds have become totems for the conservation movement. Wobbling about on land, dressed in their coat and tails and bustling about with domestic chores, they are reminiscent of miniature butlers; and like any good butler, they are much more respectable than us.

WILD DOG

The San revered the wild dog as the world's best hunter, and incorporated the animal into their mythology. From one story we learn that the moon set a pack of wild dogs to chase a hare that had disagreed with its intention to reincarnate all living things. Why the hare was such a spoilsport, and whether the dogs ever succeeded in catching it, is not ours to know.

Some elements of this story recall "The Wild Hunt," an ancient legend belonging to the tribes of northern Europe. Frequently reworked and retold, it is now so worn as to constitute an incomprehensible puzzle. The streamlined version involves a ghostly horde of horsemen and spectral hounds traversing a moonlit sky in mad pursuit of, well, nothing in particular in most cases. A Cornish version of the story provides us with a name for the intimidating canine component of this scary group: the Devil's dandy dogs.

"The Devil's dog" is an unfortunate sobriquet still sometimes applied to African wild dogs. It would probably have been the description of choice for the British big-game hunter RCF Maugham. Writing in 1914, he described wild dogs as an abomination, and fervently hoped for their complete extermination.

Despite the quasi-religious intensity of feeling, the main source of Mr. Maugham's wrath and righteous indignation probably had more to do with the dogs' atrocious table manners than to any links they may have had with the Devil. His profession involved shooting animals, big and small, and then sticking their heads up on the wall, so it's unlikely that he had a queasy stomach. But to see wild dogs tear a living impala limb from limb, without even using serviettes, was simply beyond the pale.

To deflect opprobrium, today many folk prefer to call them African painted dogs; they point out that there is ample evidence that their prey sometimes dies a quicker death than animals that fall victim to lions and leopards. These upstanding cat carnivores have the claws and dental equipment to kill by various means, most usually strangulation; but unless they get it exactly right, this can be quite a protracted process. The cats' methods are certainly less gory but often far from instantaneous.

Nevertheless, until well into the 20th century most people tended to share Mr. Maugham's views and wild dogs were routinely exterminated wherever they were found. Other factors, including loss of habitat and susceptibility to diseases such as distemper and rabies, weighed in to put the dogs firmly on the road to extinction. They are now mainly confined to the largest game reserves in East and Southern Africa, and are less frequently seen than their big-cat competitors.

To follow their preferred lifestyle, a pack of wild dogs needs a big space to move around in. Their ranges can extend up to a whopping 2,000 square kilometers (1200 square miles), though they're usually less than half of that. On bright nights they will sometimes make use of the light of the moon, but wild dogs hunt by sight and are hence mainly diurnal. Day or night, as the San undoubtedly observed, their kill rate, estimated at 85 percent of targeted animals, is much more impressive than any posted by the big cats. Down at the bottom of the class, cheetahs, in particular, look like prime candidates for extra lessons. In consequence, where game is relatively abundant the dogs are able to work on a flexitime basis and spend the hottest parts of the day collapsed in a sociable heap, amiably sharing the shade and the ever-present flies.

Be it business or pleasure, wild dogs seem to get along so well, and exude such a footloose and fancy-free vibe, that it took naturalists a long while to work out that there is, in fact, a formal hierarchy. Each pack has an alpha pair, and they are the only two who are supposed to breed. Every now and again, in larger packs, a lower-ranking female admits to having an illicit affair by dumping a set of pups in everyone's lap. When this happens, the alpha male suddenly remembers he left something important at the waterhole, and everyone else holds their breath and waits to see what the alpha female will do. She might kill the pups, adopt them, or leave the birth mother to nurse them in peace. She usually chooses the second or third option.

Nursing is no small task because an average litter is enormous by carnivore standards, sometimes numbering up to 20 pups. There's a sombre reason for this bounty: wild dogs may live a merry life by bushveld standards, but it's usually brutally short. Very few dogs live beyond five years, falling victim to lions, snares, disease and fights for dominance, or rare battles with rival packs. The result is that each pack has a high turnover of individuals. Its coherence and integrity rests in the here and now, rather than in longevity.

The dogs themselves spend no time moping about tomorrow and, despite superficial appearances, are very well organized. A pack member, slow on the hunt, may be delegated to look after pups at the den, or to perform the functions of a medic, continually licking the wounds of an injured colleague to help stave off infection. At the scene of a kill, some members are charged with keeping watch and, as needs be, every pack member coughs up lunch for pups at the den. Unlike lions at a carcass, adult wild dogs immediately make way for juveniles too young to have participated in the hunt.

None of these skills and character traits matches what the Devil generally looks for in an employee. Even with their elegant long legs and fetching tricolor coats, it's highly unlikely that they'd be able to secure a position with the diabolical dandy dogs; but Mr. Maugham's CV? Well, that's another story.

HADEDA

Ibises had the run of the place in Ancient Egypt. Nobody minded where they went or what they got up to. They could stroll through the inner sanctum of temples, the Pharaoh's private quarters or anywhere else they fancied. They could even poop on the gleaming apex of the Great Pyramid and no one would make a fuss. The reason for this unusual tolerance was that causing the death of a sacred ibis, even by accident, was a capital offense.

When Egyptian sages constructed their strange and complicated cosmology, they decided that the ibis was an earthly manifestation of the deity Thoth. Representations of the god took the form of a human body with the head of an ibis. This may have looked utterly ridiculous but only the gods could excuse someone who burst out laughing, and they wouldn't have been amused.

Thoth himself was certainly no laughing matter, having basically put the universe together. He was the true and original author of everything anyone could ever conceive. He also officiated at the weighing of souls ceremony and eternal damnation awaited anyone whose soul, when placed on the celestial scales, weighed more than a feather.

All this is perhaps worth bearing in mind if you feel inclined to throw rocks at a flock of hadedas when they start calling from the top of a tree outside your bedroom window first thing in the morning. They may be a little smaller, less dramatic and generally not as posh as the sacred ibis, but the two are close cousins and can sometimes be found sharing a lawn or seashore within gossiping distance of each other. It's perhaps best not to become one of their topics of conversation.

The hadeda's name is onomatopoeic, derived from its raucous and distinctive voice. People prefer "hadeda" to the species' scientific name, *Bostrychia hagedash*, because nobody wants to sound inebriated by pronouncing that mouthful.

The birds are widely distributed in sub-Saharan Africa, and their numbers and range have both increased substantially since the 1960s, particularly in South Africa. Part of the reason is that humans have modified the environment in ways that admirably suit the birds' lifestyle. Ibises feed by repeatedly poking their long, curved beaks into soft earth in search of worms, spiders, insects and insect larvae. So farmlands, golf courses, parks and large suburban gardens, all well irrigated and usually within easy reach of mature tall trees, are heaven-sent. They repay the hospitality by getting rid of snails and other pestilential insects, notably subterranean species that like to make a mess of lawns.

A bonus for the birds in the suburbs is that many folk keep pampered and overfed pooches as pets. A hadeda isn't interested in becoming a dog's next best friend, of course, but it is interested in the contents of its food bowl. They can become quite possessive of a particular bowl, chasing away other birds that are tempted to muscle in on the seemingly inexhaustible supply of nutritionally balanced free meals. Whether this unusual diet puts a spring in their step or a gloss on their coats has not been determined.

Tall trees are an important part of the suburban mix because they enable the birds to get safely away from trouble, including, no doubt, irate dogs that have finally woken up to what the birds have been up to. Hadedas forage in pairs or small groups during the day, but as night approaches they often congregate in large flocks and roost in the same large dormitory tree night after night, often year after year, if they're not disturbed and the local pickings are good. Their arrival and departure is invariably accompanied by one of the loudest rackets known in the avian world.

Although they're gregarious for most of the year, when spring comes around, and it's time to raise a family, the birds like privacy. Unlike the sacred ibis, which nests in communes, hadedas prefer to find their own tree, ideally on the banks of a river or a stream. In urban environments they might choose a man-made structure, provided they can find a suitable spot between 3 and 6 meters (3.2-6.5 yards) above ground.

As part of his mating display, the male bird shows bits and pieces of vegetation to the female, presumably as evidence of his prowess in construction. Duly impressed, she then helps him build an untidy platform of sticks, padded with a thin layer of lichens and grass. The nest wouldn't win any prizes for quality or comfort, let alone engineering expertise. In fact, it is usually such a shoddy piece of work that eggs or newborn chicks often topple out and are lost. It's not the end of the world because the female can lay up to six eggs. The big surprise is that the birds pair for life, and often proudly return to the same ramshackle nest the following year. The Ancient Egyptians, renowned for their precision building, would no doubt be aghast.

PYTHON

Pythons need no introduction, least of all if you find yourself inadvertently sharing a toilet with one in the African bush—or even in a bathroom in England. On such embarrassing occasions the best policy is to quickly pull up your pants, mutter an apology and retreat—or, better still, run screaming to your mother. This option was understandably selected by a young boy in the English county of Essex when he discovered a small python peering up at him from the bowl of the family toilet.

Other than its obvious function, a stylish ceramic bowl filled with cool water is just the thing for a python to wrap around on a hot summer's day or night, and having a flexible backbone with 133 vertebrae certainly helps in getting comfortable. If you're below a certain size, it's even possible to plunge in and explore the linkages in the neighborhood plumbing, as the slippery little individual in the toilet in Essex was presumably doing. Scuba diving equipment is unnecessary because they can hold their breath under water for a very long time—up to an hour if necessary.

Pythons like to keep their body temperature just below 32 degrees centigrade (89.6 degrees fahrenheit), so when they start to feel too hot they seek shade, go underground, slide into a rock crevice or into the nearest river or dam. Heading for a bathroom is not usually an option, but in an increasingly crowded and careless world, where exotic pets are not uncommon, it can happen more often than people think.

An African python that managed to escape into the suburbs of Essex would struggle to survive the vagaries of an English summer, let alone a bitter winter. If it somehow did, and fortuitously bumped into a fellow escapee of the opposite sex, breeding successfully would prove virtually impossible. Python eggs need to be kept warm, above 28 degrees centigrade (82.4 degrees fahrenheit), to give them any chance of hatching. Even in Africa, brooding southern African pythons often need to bask in the sun, allowing their body temperature to rise to dangerous levels so that they can then curl around their eggs and transfer the warmth. That's impossible on a soggy weekend in Southend-on-Sea.

There are, however, more benign places where escaped or released pythons have prospered, including one of the world's leading depositories of unwanted exotic fauna: the Florida Everglades. African pythons are hugely outnumbered there by Burmese pythons, but it's still early days. The Burmese have settled in wonderfully, and gotten to know the indigenous neighbors so well that they frequently have them for lunch. Life in the Everglades, for the moment at least, is actually an improvement on their natural home in Southeast Asia, where things haven't been going at all well for pythons lately. One of the reasons is that well over 100,000 have been yanked out of their natural habitat by dealers in recent years, and shipped off to the USA as pets.

Not that they're bragging about it, but African rock pythons can grow a little bigger than their Burmese cousins, capable of surpassing a length of 5 meters (16 feet), if they live long enough. The biggest weigh in the vicinity of 60 kilograms (132 pounds), at least between meals. These behemoths can gulp down an animal as big as an impala or a wild dog. After such a huge meal the snake is, of course, suddenly a great deal heavier, and it can take a couple of weeks to get back to sensible proportions. In the immediate aftermath, the rotund snake is itself vulnerable, not just to fat

jokes, but also to predators with a taste for stuffed snake, with a surprise side dish of marinated impala. While the meal is being digested, the snake understandably tries to stay well hidden in a burrow or dense undergrowth.

Being uniquely equipped to pig out doesn't necessarily mean that every meal has to consist of a jaw-stretching mountain of meat. Everyone does their best when the man from the Guinness Book of Records is watching, but even the biggest pythons sometimes choose fairly modest portions—a dassie, a duck, or even, for the particularly daring, a prickly porcupine. On the whole, pythons have a preference for warm-blooded prey but they're certainly not averse to making selections from the cold buffet: monitor lizards, young crocodiles, and fish when available.

Pythons are cold blooded themselves, a state commonly equated to being heartless, and yet they're famous for their tight embraces. Not everyone who comes along can expect a big hug of course, and by and large the snakes remain aloof, invariably slipping away unobtrusively if disturbed while out in the open. Even their nuptials are civilized by animal standards. Any number of eager males will follow the scent trail laid down by a receptive female, but fights never happen.

Relatively recent research has revealed that, despite seeming implacable, cold and uncaring, some female African pythons actually look after their young, at least after a fashion. When the eggs hatch they don't simply breathe a serpentine sigh of relief and immediately slip away, as previously thought. Instead, the mother stays in attendance for three or four weeks, perhaps a lot longer, providing body warmth for the brood at night and deterring predators simply by being there. What is more surprising is that the young, like all newborn snakes well able to fend for themselves, choose to stay with her. It can't be for the free meals because there aren't any.

VLEI RAT

Tourism promoters don't usually go out of their way to brag about the rat-viewing opportunities available in their country or region. They would rather devote space in their glossy brochures to airbrushed images of snarling leopards, yawning lions and bellicose elephants. Even guidebooks tend to assume that anyone weird enough to want to look at rats in their natural habitat can find their own way to the garbage cans in the alley behind their hotel.

A prevalent, albeit uncritical, view is that rats virtually invented dirt and disease. The periodic plagues that nearly wipe out humanity are routinely blamed on them. They are more toxic than nuclear waste and spend their time in sewers and dark cellars, plotting to take over the world.

Sharing a name with a creature like that would make anyone afraid to show their face in public. Fortunately, the vlei rat has always lived out in the country and is happily unaware of the opprobrium generously and indiscriminately heaped upon its extended family. It's not fond of showing its face anyway, because there's always a chance that a marsh owl or a patrolling serval cat will spot it, and that can end in disaster. Owl pellets, in some areas, tend to be liberally peppered with the fractured remains of inattentive rats.

Vlei rats prefer to live in dense grasslands associated with the wetlands and marshes of temperate and sub-tropical areas, mainly in southern and eastern South Africa. By their nature, such environments tend to be fragmented and the rat cannot easily pack its bags and move on in search of another life. There is thus little need to interrupt its simple world with the cautionary tales of degradation and debauchery that befell its distant cousins in the city.

A healthy outdoor lifestyle has contributed to these strict vegetarians being moderately large by rat standards, though still only about 16 centimeters (6 inches) in length, with another 10 centimeters (4 inches) added on for the tail. Home is a modest grass saucer hidden in dense vegetation, and located a meter (yard) or so above any foreseeable flood level. They can swim well, if they must, but generally prefer traveling on the well-worn footpaths radiating out from their cozy nest. The only things missing from this idyllic neighborhood are elves with buttercup lanterns to light the way at night. The moon helps, when it's in the mood but, by and large, vlei rats conduct the bulk of their business during the day.

They are not known for their dazzling social skills, often preferring to lead a solitary life. In consequence they are usually a little cranky with strangers of their own kind and bloody fights are not unknown. To stave off an attack, the accepted procedure is to stand erect on one's rear feet, exposing the tummy, and make little twittering noises. Nuptial arrangements tend to be fairly flighty affairs, and although long-term relationships have been noted in some communities, these appear to be the exception rather than the rule.

Baby vlei rats are born with their coats on and their incisors erupted. The three or four infants clamp their little teeth to their mother's teats and cling on tenaciously whenever she leaves the nest to go about her daily chores. They're able to eat solid food within two or three days, but the eye-watering nipple routine continues for about two weeks, by which time they're fully weaned—no doubt to an audible sigh of relief. Young vlei rats grow rapidly and in less than three months they're sexually mature. It may all seem unnecessarily hectic and rushed, but if you're a vlei rat, it's important to get on with life, because it will all be over in a couple of years.

Although not immediately endangered, their chosen habitat is increasingly under threat, both from climate change and the remorseless growth in human numbers. The edges of wetlands are continuously nibbled away or simply gobbled whole to facilitate new agricultural and mining developments or housing projects. Vlei rats rarely, if ever, encounter their brown rat distant cousins. If and when they did, the meeting would probably take place on a landfill, against the background roar of bulldozers and dump trucks. We can only wonder what the city rats would tell their country cousins about us. It is unlikely to be anything good.

COCKROACH

Nobody knows exactly when the supercontinent of Gondwana broke in half, creating Africa and South America, but the best guess is about 100 million years ago. If cockroaches could talk—and had bothered to keep a diary—they would be able to tell us precisely when it happened, because they witnessed the whole thing, from both sides of the big divide.

By then they were already an old species—so ancient, in fact, that they had ringside seats when the even bigger monocontinent of Pangaea broke asunder. That was about 200 million years ago, but here again, we don't have any diary notes, so it's difficult to be absolutely precise.

At least the rocks made some sort of effort, and the fossil record is fairly up to date. From this we can ascertain that cockroaches have been around for a mind-numbingly long time, well over 300 million years. Charles Darwin referred to them as "living fossils," meaning it as a compliment, a rare thing in itself from a member of the human race. Cockroaches are generally reviled as disgusting vermin, but Darwin recognized their impressive lineage, and the perfection of their simple and practical shape.

Although there's been ample time to tinker, the cockroach's basic design has always remained the same. In essence it consists of a head, thorax and abdomen, is bilaterally symmetrical, and flat and ovoid in shape. A hard helmet, known as a pronotum, protects the head. On either side of the body there are three legs and, up front, a pair of impressive antennae. The three body segments are encased in a hard exoskeleton, which in turn is covered with a slippery outer skin. This last layer prevents the cockroach from becoming dehydrated, and helps it to slide in and out of impossibly tight spaces.

The exoskeleton is punctured by spiracles, or small holes, to facilitate breathing, and housed within it is a sophisticated and complex chemical plant. This produces all kinds of chemical cocktails, used to regulate virtually every aspect of the creature's interactions with the outside world, including with others of its own kind.

If all this sounds like the description of some sort of space suit, that's probably no coincidence. The cockroach is kitted out to function in extremely hostile environments, and it has certainly seen them come and go. Being around when the continents broke apart, like bits of crumbly fudge, must have been disconcerting. But over the eons the insects have had to contend with a range of climactic and geological catastrophes, many of them causing the mass extinction of other species. The meteorite strike, which so befouled the planet that the dinosaurs decided to call it a day, was but one.

An atmosphere thick with soot and atomized saurian body parts may have been problematic, but cockroaches had already survived earlier conditions, when the air was so rich in oxygen that their predators were able to grow to ridiculous proportions. In the Devonian, dragonflies were the size of eagles, and carnivorous centipedes were big enough to trip up an elephant. For the cockroach, then as now, a typical day at the office has never been uneventful.

As all astronauts and professional deep-sea divers know, if you want to survive in a hostile environment, you need to keep checking your equipment. Above all, it's important to make sure everything is clean, so it will work perfectly. For just this reason, and contrary to popular opinion, cockroaches are scrupulous about their personal hygiene. Each long antenna has 365 segments, each responsible for monitoring some aspect of the bug's environment, including its own cleanliness and aroma. If you turn on the kitchen light at night and see a cockroach, there's a fair chance that it's cleaner than the floor.

A few species seem to prefer being in and around human habitations; they are also adept at hitching rides on various forms of transport, keen to join us wherever we may be, including in Antarctica. South Africa boasts several immigrant species, including the American cockroach, *Periplaneta americana*. They are particularly loathed, and yet extremely comfortable in Durban, having shipped in from the USA in times long past. Some African roaches have traveled the other way, to an equally hostile reception in American cities.

We tend to flatter ourselves that roach armies are squarely focused on us, dependent on our handouts, no matter how reluctantly given. It may be a comfort to bear in mind that there are over 4,500 species of cockroach alive today, and only 30 of them are generally regarded as pests. These ignoble few are very good at exploiting our built environments and taking advantage of the messes we make, but the vast majority don't want anything to do with the human race. They make their living in virtually every ecological niche, from tropical forests to swamps, deserts and grasslands.

Out in the wild, perched on rotting tree trunks or lichen-covered rocks, it may be that at this very moment cockroaches are waving their antennae and sensing a change in the wind; noxious gases and atmospheric anomalies, subtle murmurs of another impending global catastrophe. If just one of them has managed to get hold of a diary, this may be a good time to start taking notes.

SPRINGHARE

Exasperated scientists may have booted it into its own genus, but the springhare can at least lay a tenuous claim to being the model for a popular American icon. Anyone familiar with the stories of Brer Rabbit is likely to know that the original folktales featuring this dodgy, but lovable, character were brought to the southern states by African slaves. Some now suggest that the tales originated in Angola, and are based not on the rabbit, but on the springhare, an artful dodger if ever there was one.

Springhares are neither rabbits nor hares, and, despite appearances, nor are they any kind of miniature kangaroo. They are, in fact, rodents. All the confusion is entirely attributable to nature's habit of patting herself on the back and then repeating elements of a clever design.

The creatures themselves must surely have their own opinion regarding nature's brilliance at the drawing board, especially when it's time for bed. To get comfortable in the confines of a narrow burrow, they need to tuck their head between their outsized rear legs and enormous feet, and rest their forehead on the ground. It must be like trying to doze off in economy class wearing a pair of clown shoes. Getting comfortable is important because springhares, being nocturnal, spend the whole day like that.

Most bushveld creatures needing subterranean accommodation make do with relatively capacious old aardvark burrows. Springhares have their own ideas and prefer to dig their own home, or rather homes, because they normally have more than one address. They end up being rather modest constructions, simple tunnels without chambers, larders or discernible toilets.

The springhare's front paws are equipped with strong claws, but the animal is nevertheless fairly petite, and hence needs to find an area of soft, compacted sand to work with; clay soils, baked red earth and rocky terrain are too much of a challenge. In consequence, although the species is widely distributed, from southern Kenya down to South Africa, individual populations are patchy.

Favored habitats are sandy areas in the savanna, preferably dry and certainly not too wet or cold—and without too many boulders, trees and prickly bushes. With a nit-picking, *prima donna* attitude like that, you could be forgiven for thinking that springhares must be teetering on the edge of extinction, or at least ought to be. In fact, they're doing rather well, despite briefly featuring on the The International Union for Conservation of Nature's Vulnerable (IUCNs) list not so very long ago. They've since bounced back from that.

Bouncing out of trouble is what life's mostly about for a springhare. They can cover 3 meters (10 feet) in a single hop, enough to get them instantly out of reach of the claws or the jaws of a predator. They certainly need the practice: the queue of animals itching to eat one would stretch right around the landscape's fattest baobab, and even down to the rock on the corner. Everyone's there: snakes, eagles, honey badgers, leopards, lions, jackals, wild dogs, civets—even some of the vegetarians look as though they're having a lifestyle rethink. It is little wonder these hares spend the daylight hours tucked away in a tube underground, the entrance plugged from within. When they do emerge, after dark, they sometimes shoot out like furry little cannonballs, just in case there's something ferocious waiting at the entrance.

Assuming they can avoid the slobbering queue of potential assassins, springhares spend the night quietly shuffling about on all fours looking for their own sustenance. They enjoy seeds, leaves, berries, succulent stems and even the occasional grasshopper. When they find a choice item, they clasp it in their front paws, sit back on their haunches and nibble; in this pose they look—I have to say it—a bit like large squirrels. They obtain virtually all their water requirements from the food they eat.

Springhares prefer their own company, though natural restrictions in available living and foraging space can mean that large numbers end up cheek by jowl in the same neighborhood; even their tunnels can inadvertently interlink, and goodness knows what then goes on underground, away from prying eyes. They can become so numerous in some areas that the reflection from the eyes of a mob of springhares caught in headlamps as they feed in the veld at night has been likened to city lights.

Exceptionally for a rodent, springhares don't believe in having big families, restricting themselves to one bouncing baby at a time. And, probably mindful of the kid's big feet and the cramped nature of her living quarters, the mother alone looks after the infant. But springhares do breed year round and a female can produce three offspring in a year, so in theory a local population can increase quite rapidly. This reckons, of course, without the horde of hungry diners, including *Homo sapiens*, nature's most prominent queue jumper.

Springhares traditionally formed an important part of the diet of many African tribes, most notably the San, and they all made good use of the skins for karosses, clothing and water containers. Ending up as a water bottle is an odd fate for an animal that rarely, if ever, took a drink while alive.

CARACAL

A caracal recently caught on camera killing 20 African penguins near Cape Town was probably hoping the blame would be pinned on a lynx. The two look alike, at least at a glance, in dim light, with clouds across the moon. Local law enforcement could be faced with a genuine conundrum if not for the fact that the nearest lynx lives in Spain.

Despite their similarity in size, and the natty tufts of hair on their ears, the two cats are only distantly related. The caracal has been around a long time, eight million years or more, while the lynx is a much newer evolutionary addition to the feline family. The caracal's closest cousin isn't the lynx, but rather the African Golden Cat, which will no doubt also claim that it was nowhere near the penguin colony at the time.

Nevertheless, as far as nomenclature is concerned, confusion reigns and has for as long as anyone can't remember. Caracals owe their name to the kind of sloppy pronunciation that happens when cultures collide and coalesce. The Turks called the cat *kara kulak*, which means "black ear," and the word bumbled into English as "caracal." Prior to that, in the Middle Ages, everyone thought they were lynxes, because that's what the Romans and the brainy Ancient Greeks had called them; in fact, any cat bigger than the humble domestic pussy, and smaller than a lion or a leopard, was often called a lynx.

Reluctant to let go of a punchy name, many folk in South Africa still call the caracal a lynx, while a select few elevate the cats to a higher, double-barreled social stratum, and call it a caracal-lynx. The Afrikaners, refusing to get embroiled in the controversy, call it a *rooikat*.

Caracals are endemic to Africa, the Middle East, India and Southeast Asia, but they're faring a lot better in some places than others, largely depending upon the pressures exerted by burgeoning human populations. In India they're endangered, while in Africa they're particularly widespread, ranging from the slopes of Table Mountain to the Nile valley in Egypt.

They're usually associated with relatively dry habitats, woodlands and savannas, but happily slot into a variety of ecosystems, from forest to semi-desert. The mountainous region of South Africa's Eastern Cape province purportedly has one of the highest population densities. Over in the west, in and around the leafy suburbs bordering the nature reserves that make up the Table Mountain National Park, the cats are experimenting with semi-urban living, so much so that they've started to feature in road accident statistics. Caracals killed while crossing suburban roads are mostly young males, which are much more peripatetic than females.

Despite the automotive dangers, peripheral city life has its advantages. Rodents discovered ages ago that there's an excellent living to be had around human beings, particularly urbanites; they're such messy and wasteful eaters. It's therefore unsurprising that abundant rats and mice, a favorite prey species, feature prominently in the diet of Cape metro caracals. Also available, as an occasional delicacy, are domestic cats—at least those brave or daft enough to tiptoe beyond the manicured lawns and well-trimmed hedges of suburbia into the edges of neighboring wild lands.

Caracals can lay claim to the dubious distinction of being the original cat among the pigeons. In days gone by, potentates in Persia and India used tame caracals to hunt game, typically small mammals and birds. As an entertaining sideline, they enjoyed releasing one of the springy cats into a large room full of pigeons, placing bets on how many it could pluck from the air in a set time. The record, according to anecdotal evidence, was 12.

Propelled by powerful hindquarters, caracals are capable of truly extraordinary leaps, 3 meters (10 feet) straight up from a squatting start. Despite applying max flaps and full thrust, a guinea fowl flushed from the grass has little chance of escaping. But adept as they are at jumping, an aerial intercept is not the caracal's standard hunting method. Like others of their kind, they're ambush predators, making use of cover until they're close enough to charge or pounce.

Caracals aren't too fussy about what's on the menu, provided it's made of meat. Unlike jackals, they're strictly carnivorous, and definitely not available to share a bowl of berries. Insects and lizards are fine as canapés, but their main day-to-day fare consists of rodents, small mammals, typically dassies and duiker-sized antelope, and birds as big as bustards. There are recorded instances of hefty caracals successfully bringing down ostrich and even adult antelope.

Jackals, which often share the same turf, are a pain in the furry butt as far as caracals are concerned. The two species indulge in tit-for-tat baby snatching (and crunching and munching) so it's little wonder that they loathe each other. As with lions, which seem to deliberately seek out and destroy cheetah cubs in the Serengeti, this behavior may have as much to do with eliminating competition as seeking sustenance.

Whatever caracals choose to hunt, they hunt alone. With the exception of mothers raising kittens, they lead a solitary life, and mainly inhabit the night. There is some evidence that this nocturnal lifestyle is driven by self-preservation rather than choice; in areas of scant or non-existent human populations, notably remote parts of Turkey and Arabia, they are just as likely to be out and about during the day. But hunting at night does have its advantages: there's a better than even chance that a prospective meal has nodded off. A caracal can shoot up a tree in the blink of a bleary eye to grab a small monkey or a roosting bird.

Not that such lethal efficiency impresses everyone. As the occasional perpetrators of excessive and bloody mass slaughters, caracals are regarded by some folk, notably chicken and sheep farmers, as the devil incarnate. While African penguins might be persuaded to testify, albeit reluctantly, that such abhorrent behavior is rare, when it does occur, caracals, like leopards, are judged in human terms. All too often, this leads to a highly poisonous and grossly indiscriminate human response.

CUCKOO

In his handbook on elementary clock making, written in 1669, Domenico Martinelli proposed that the call of a cuckoo be used to indicate the passing hours.

Being a medieval European, it's unlikely that Mr. Martinelli was familiar with the call of the Piet-my-vrou, more formally known as the red-chested cuckoo, a species native to Africa. If he had been, and had lain awake long enough on a moonlit night, sleepless on account of its monotonous and ceaseless call, he would certainly have reconsidered his proposal; he would probably have gone outside in his pajamas at two o'clock in the morning, and thrown his handbook in the direction of the maddening sound.

Ornithologists have yet to work out exactly what point the Piet-my-vrou is trying to make with its repetitive babble, and to whom. However, there is general consensus, at least in southern Africa, that the cuckoo's name is applied to fools and the insane for good reason. The bird arrives each summer from central Africa, perches high in the canopy of tall trees, all but invisible, and sets about calling—for mind-numbing hours on end, day or night—for new recruits for the dippidy-doo club.

The Piet-my-vrou is nevertheless more infamous, like all cuckoos, for laying its eggs in the nests of other birds, invariably ones much smaller than itself. Its favored foster parents are Cape robins but an assortment of dupes, including wagtails and thrushes, may be selected for the dubious honor. Some species of cuckoo are specialists, tailoring their eggs in terms of color and size to match those of a specific host bird, but the Piet-my-vrou isn't too bothered about producing exact replicas. Cape robins don't seem to be good at math, and would probably struggle to agree on a new shade of beige for the lounge curtains.

For a couple of lazy bastards, a pair of Piet-my-vrous set about their duplicitous scheme with surprising thoroughness. They first scout out the neighborhood for suitable nests. When they find one, the female cuckoo lurks nearby, taking note, like a sleazy private eye, of the comings and goings of the happy resident couple. Timing is everything and only once the prospective host bird has laid her eggs does the male cuckoo call to distract her from her nest. The plucky little mother promptly slips out to see off the intruder and the female cuckoo darts in. She needs only 5 to 10 seconds on the nest and the deed is done.

From the sidelines, it seems strange that they've gotten away with it for so long, but that's not always the case. Sometimes they're found out and the egg is disposed of or the nest abandoned. A recent study by Spain's University of Granada has revealed that the great spotted cuckoo, which has traditionally palmed off its eggs on magpies, doesn't always even wait for the host bird to leave the nest. Magpies have apparently become wise to their game and tend to stay put on their eggs, so a brazen approach has become necessary. The magpie understandably makes a huge fuss as the cuckoo barges in and positions its ample posterior over her nest; but amid all the pecking, flapping and general excitement, she seems to lose track of what's really happening, so the cuckoo often still gets away with it.

Cuckoos are not the only birds that dodge parental responsibilities. The cowbird of Central America lays an egg in the ornate hanging nest carefully constructed by the chestnut-headed oropendola. Unashamedly, she boots the reluctant hostess off the cot so that she can get comfortable. But at least there's a payoff for both parties: cowbird chicks are precocious and, from the moment they hatch, gobble up visiting botflies, which would otherwise lay their eggs in the flesh of the helpless oropendola chicks, usually with fatal results. In locales where botflies are absent, the oropendolas are far less accommodating, and the cowbird has to resort to more traditional cuckoo-type methods.

A cuckoo embryo sometimes develops more quickly and so has a head start inside its egg, and usually hatches before the host's chicks are ready to peck their way out of their shells. Within moments of emerging, the young cuckoo sets about heaving the host's eggs—or even the other chicks, if they have inconveniently put in an appearance—up and out of the nest. Despite the fact that it's a downright nasty thing to do, one has to admire the newborn's strength and determination. It's the physical equivalent of a week-old human infant clambering out of its crib to do the laundry or clear out the garage.

It's clear that nature, far from being indignant, aides and abets the cuckoo's reprehensible lifestyle. The newborn of most species imprint themselves on whoever they perceive to be their parents, which can lead to ludicrous and comical situations, but young cuckoos never suffer any such identity crisis. When they've finished sponging off their diminutive foster parents, they know exactly who they really are and where they belong.

When it's good and ready, a Piet-my-vrou heads north to winter in central Africa without so much as a begrudging thanks to its exhausted hosts. It will duly return the following spring, often to the locale where it was born, and team up with a mate for another spin on their warped and wobbly version of the cycle of life.

VERVET MONKEY

When you're far from home, highly-strung and growing up in a strange land, the temptation to hit the bottle is an ever-present danger. This probably explains why immigrant vervet monkeys, scattered in small populations across the balmy islands of the Caribbean, have a teenage drinking problem. Their sober forbears arrived from Africa on slave ships, carried along for the amusement of the crew, and on arrival escaped into a tropical countryside rapidly being transformed into one humongous sugar cane plantation.

Fermenting sugar produces ethanol, a substance familiar to brewers and manufacturers of fine wines, whiskeys and rotgut the world over. It is mainly young vervet monkeys that can't resist a tipple; as they get older a sense of social responsibility seems to take over and adults largely go on the wagon.

Given this penchant for substance abuse, it's probably little wonder that vervets have long been a favorite subject for study by folk trying to figure out why humans behave as they do. They're very like us in other ways, susceptible to the same and similar diseases and inclined to suffer from hypertension. If it were not for a long-ago roll of the evolutionary dice, one of them might be writing this and I could instead be sitting on the branch of a marula tree, fretting about life and waiting for nature to open the bar.

Being relatively easy to handle and breed in captivity, they have played an important role in biomedical research, notably into HIV/AIDS, and have reluctantly though laudably contributed to the production of smallpox and polio vaccines.

Vervets are members of the genus *Chlorocebus*, and various subspecies, some six in all, live all over Africa with the exception of the heavily forested Congo Basin, which is dark, dangerous and not the kind of place you want to spend the night in. With the exception of coat color, which varies between subtle shades of brown and gray, they all look pretty much alike.

Their preferred habitat is lightly wooded savanna, riverine woodlands and coastal scrub but they're highly adaptable, making a modest living in cultivated lands and sometimes, where modern realities dictate it, in suburbia. Their relationship with the local human inhabitants is not always cordial, especially when open windows and well-stocked kitchens are involved. Nevertheless, they're relatively harmless and the males' brief macho displays invariably evaporate into flight at the close approach of an irate human. Like any other animal they will fight back if cornered or attacked, and have a respectable pair of canines to bring to the party.

Adult male vervets tip the scales at about 6 kilograms (13 pounds), on average, and females are about a kilo lighter (about 10-11 pounds), so they're not really in a position to throw their weight around. Instead they seek security in numbers, forming troops of between 20 and 50 individuals. They've developed about 30 distinct alarm calls to alert each other to the presence of different predators, including, it seems, an appropriate and probably unprintable epithet for *Homo sapiens*. Main wild threats come from leopards, large raptors, big butch snakes and baboons, the warning call for each eliciting a particular behavioral response.

Each troop has its undemocratically elected leader, invariably the largest, loudest and most politically astute male. He earns and maintains his status by fighting, pulling scary faces and making and discarding alliances as it suits him. A second-in-command assists him. This worthy's duties include scouting out foraging sites and keeping his eyes and ears open for danger. Only the leader of the troop gets to mate, which helps explain why young males tend to move between troops, probably hoping that a change of scene will improve their career and hence their prospects for romance.

The birth of a vervet monkey is a major event in the social calendar and all troop members are eager to inspect the baby. When it is two to three weeks old, adolescent females help care for the infant, sometimes enthusiastically snatching the bawling baby from its mother's weary arms. A close and intriguing bond often develops between a young vervet and its grandmother. Granny always has time for junior and studies seem to show that this has a direct impact on the infant survival rate, which at the best of times is statistically no better than 50/50.

While young males are of necessity mobile, female vervets usually remain within the same troop their whole lives. They are born into a relatively rigid hierarchy headed by a matriarch who keeps a snobbish note of everyone's lineage and isn't above ticking off a social upstart. Studying the family tree, so to speak, can soon reveal who is taking tea with the duchess and who's doing the washing up.

Vervets are highly territorial and boundary squabbles between troops are routine. As with us, it's all about guarding the resources necessary for survival. They're omnivorous and select from a wide menu, varying from edible leaves and fruit to grasshoppers and other insects, with the occasional bird's egg and hatchling thrown in. Given such a wide variety of seemingly ubiquitous foods, it's easy to imagine that finding something to eat poses no problem. Nevertheless, with its seasons and cycles, droughts and deluges, the African landscape can be a bleak place and life is seldom a picnic for monkeys. When the opportunity presents itself, perhaps it's little wonder that they invite themselves to our picnics and outdoor feasts, and maybe, purely by accident, knock over the wine.

RHINO

It's not known for certain when the woolly rhinoceros became extinct, or who was responsible, but the Neolithic police put out a detailed description of one of the principal suspects about 12,000 years ago. He was tall, excruciatingly thin, had a big nose, a jutting jaw, some kind of tattoo on his upper torso, and was last seen loitering in the vicinity of Creswell Crags in Derbyshire. There are additional pornographic details, which have been withheld in the name of common decency. The most incriminating piece of evidence linking him to the crime is the indisputable fact that his likeness was found carved on a woolly rhino's rib.

To be fair to Pinhole Cave Man, as he is known, woolly rhinos may actually have outnumbered him and his stick-figure chums back in Ice-Age Europe. What's more, AK-47s and helicopters hadn't been invented yet. Bringing down an animal that was the same size and configuration as a modern white rhino would have been no mean feat, especially if you were so anorexic that you could pass for a cartoon. Nevertheless, many scientists are more or less convinced that Pinhole did it, or at least tipped the balance. The final curtain fell on the woollies about 8,000 years ago.

We now find ourselves back in the dock as repeat offenders. Despite public outrage and the herculean efforts of conservationists, both species of African rhino continue to seesaw toward extinction in an unfolding tragedy that is utterly mindless. Pinhole and Co. at least had the excuse that they hunted to survive. Other than monumental stupidity and epic greed, we have none.

We used to know little about rhinos and now, in a sense, we know too much. They've been stripped of the authority and mystery that came from standing aloof and apart, like big bouncers outside an exclusive club, unapproachable and unassailable, one of the Big Five. They evolved in a time when bulk and a thick hide made it unnecessary to run away from predators. In the face of a perceived threat, a rhino's main defensive strategy has always been to charge the bastards, as Dirty Harry might succinctly have put it.

This is exactly what they did when first confronted by big-game hunters and it soon earned them a reputation for being dangerous and aggressive. In reality, white rhinos are quite placid and even amiable, providing you don't tiptoe up behind them and pop a paper bag.

Females without calves often share their home range, seeming to enjoy each other's company. Bulls stick to their own territory, happy to have the gals over but routinely seeing off rival males. They make an exception when their territory happens to control access to water in a given locale. Other males are then permitted to pass through if they're heading for a drink, provided they show proper respect. Rather incongruously, this includes curling up their little tail and conspicuously urinating in a steady stream, as opposed to the spectacular spray a bull let's fly when he's marking his boundaries.

Black rhinos are half the size and consequently not as confident; they tend to be solitary and more on edge. Within living memory, they used to be the species most commonly seen in game reserves throughout Africa but their numbers have now dropped perilously low and the few that survive try to stay hidden. The western black rhino was last glimpsed in the wilds of Cameroon in 2001, one of only five individuals of this subspecies then known to still exist. By now they have almost certainly all gone, falling foul of poachers, or are so dispersed that they haven't been able to find a mate.

Black and white rhinos diverged from a common ancestor about 4 million years ago and went their separate ways, the whites opting to become giant lawn mowers, while the blacks preferred a career in hedge and shrub trimming. Black rhinos have a pointed, hook-shaped upper lip to enable them to get a proper grip on twigs and leaves; white rhinos have wide, square lips to tackle grass. In the African garden of long ago there was ample room for both, one favoring thick bush and the other the grassy plains.

Both species remained true to the fashions presumably current in the Late Miocene and kept the same gray coat. This, of course, begs the question as to why they were described as black versus white in the first place. A favorite theory is that "white" was a corruption of *wijde*, the Dutch word for wide, and hence a reference to the white rhino's wide lips, but this has since been contested. Other theories abound and the current consensus is that nobody's really got a clue. Even if the riddle is somehow solved, the black rhino will still be waiting impatiently for its own explanation.

Or maybe not—if it has any sense it would ignore the debate and head for the nearest mud wallow, emerging to sow further confusion as a yellowish, reddish or even bluish rhino, depending upon the pigments in the soil. Mud baths are an important part of a rhino's regular routine, the slosh acting as a kind of sun screen and helping to smother and kill parasites on the animal's skin.

Routine looms large in a rhino's life, and the fact that they tend to be so predictable has always made them vulnerable to human hunters. To aid digestion, they need to drink every day and generally choose the same time of day, morning and evening, to visit the same waterhole. They usually take the same route too, along paths so well worn that they can become ditch-like in places. It's the kind of setup that any professional assassin would kill for.

In a generally hostile world, the one good friend rhinos have always been able to count on is a small bird with a colorful beak. Red- and yellow-billed oxpeckers make a living hopping about from stem to stern on their favorite rhino, eating ticks and other parasites and acting as lookouts for their myopic hosts. They spend a lot of time searching in and around the rhino's ears, seeming to whisper little secrets. Given the rate at which rhinos are disappearing, they are secrets we'll undoubtedly never share.

ALBATROSS

The albatross was inducted into the realm of the magical and mystical by the poet Samuel Taylor Coleridge. His classic poem, *The Rime of the Ancient Mariner*, tells of a disaster that overtook a ship's crew when one of them raised his bow and shot a black albatross.

As the bird dies, the wind drops, the sea settles to a dead calm, and the ship then stagnates for many dry days and weeks. In a bid to fend off the inevitable, the superstitious sailors fasten the bird's carcass around their guilty shipmate's neck. That doesn't help, though it's difficult to understand why any of them could think it might. They all die of thirst, the rotten ship goes down, and only the killer survives, compelled by fate to endlessly repeat his sorry tale to strangers equally compelled to listen.

Coleridge drew inspiration for the poem from the story of Simon Hatley, the sole survivor rescued from the wreck of the *Speedwell*, a ship that foundered in the southern ocean early in the 17th century. Hatley shot an albatross shortly before the sinking, and presumably blamed this for the subsequent disaster. By an odd twist of literary fate, at some point in his piratical career, Hatley had been a shipmate of William Dapier and Andrew Selkirk, respectively the models for Gulliver (of *Gulliver's Travels*) and *Robinson Crusoe*.

As seafarers in the southern ocean, all three men would have been familiar with the albatross and probably aware of the superstitions surrounding it. The great birds routinely followed sailing ships as they voyaged across the vast and featureless expanses of deep, cold sea. With a background chorus of wind in the rigging, it would have been easy for mariners to imagine that a big white bird circling in the twilight was really the soul of a drowned sailor. It's little wonder that the netherworld got upset if you killed one.

The real reason for the bird's close attendance is more prosaic. People on ships, then as now, routinely chuck rubbish overboard, some of it edible. Ships came to exert an even greater fascination for albatrosses, and other seabirds, when large-scale whaling and commercial fishing began in the southern ocean. Over the years and decades, huge quantities of offal were routinely dumped into the sea, and even the mighty wandering albatross was frequently seen venturing close to the southern and eastern shores of South Africa to secure its share of the bounty.

Those days of plenty are long gone, for the birds and for us, but from time to time the smaller albatrosses still hang hopefully above the stern of fishing boats. Many discover that turning up for free meals can prove expensive. Getting hooked on a baited long line is invariably fatal, and the chunkily built black-browed albatross, in particular, is still sometimes deliberately snared, and finds its way into the cooking pots of fishermen.

Scavenging food from the surface of the sea is standard practice for an albatross, especially the wandering albatross which, with a wingspan in excess of 3.5 meters (11.5 feet), is the biggest of them all. It is superbly designed to soar effortlessly through the air, but ill equipped to dive for its lunch. The bulk of its natural diet consists of squid, some captured alive when they rise at night, but most of them dead already and floating on the surface. These latter bonanzas are vomited up by overindulgent whales, or are the result of the mass mortalities associated with the squid's breeding cycle.

Some smaller species of albatross, better able to dive underwater for a meter or two (a yard or two), do specialize in fish. Within any given population, including the great albatrosses, there are really no hard-and-fast rules: if it's eatable and somehow reachable, be it krill, a hooked fish, the guts of a seal, or a shark dismembered by a killer whale, an albatross will grab it.

Albatrosses are not great wing flappers. Getting into the air is a laborious business, be it from land or the sea, and particularly so for the

heavyweights. They need a run and a good headwind to get airborne. Once up, special tendons lock their narrow outstretched wings into place, so that no further muscle energy need be expended. The birds are then largely dependent on the speed of the wind to generate the lift they need to soar and glide.

If the wind drops completely when an albatross is far out over the ocean, it has little option but to drop down onto the surface and wait for the next strong breeze. Bobbing about on the water, the bird is immediately vulnerable to sharks and other marine predators, including, one presumes, the occasional vengeful giant squid.

Mercifully, they never suffer the same fate as the Ancient Mariner and his shipmates. An albatross has its own on-board desalination plant, as do penguins and many other marine birds. It can drink seawater and then expel the salt through its nasal passages.

The need for strong and predictable winds helps explain why most species of albatross, including the greats, live in southern latitudes. The Roaring Forties and Furious Fifties were so named for good reason: what is invariably a loud and scary nightmare for lone round-the-world yachtsmen is music to the ears of an albatross. The constant circumpolar winds, and the giant waves they generate, provide perfect conditions for the albatross's soaring and gliding aerial lifestyle. Albatrosses routinely zoom around the bottom of the world, up and over the big rolling waves south of Africa, Australia and South America. Throughout the trip they barely flap their wings, and their heartbeat stays constant, as if they were back on their nest.

Albatrosses breed communally, mainly on isolated islands in the far south, with different species often happily coexisting on the same remote piece of hummocky real estate. Young birds don't recklessly take the plunge with the opposite sex, but rather experiment with different dates in the flamboyant and complex dancing rituals for which the species is renowned. Several seasons may pass before a bird finds the perfect fit for its unique style of bill clacking, preening, neck stretching and calling to the sky. Finally satisfied that their opposite number isn't a weirdo, the happy couple mate and then generally stay together for life.

Life can be a long time for an albatross, upwards of 40 years, and in some recorded instances a great deal longer than that. During all that time they soar above the desolate southern ocean, covering a total distance which, if laid out in a straight line, would take them far beyond the moon.

MARABOU STORK

Most folk think that Marilyn Monroe had nothing in common with the ugliest bird in the world, and they are, of course, right. Except for those feathers. The marabou stork and Ms. Monroe shared that cozy little secret. She occasionally wore them to adorn her shoes and, quite probably, her unmentionables, whereas the marabou wears them, or rather grows them, on its tail.

Down feathers from the marabou are a sought-after item in the fashion industry, mainly used to create feather boas, and to add frills to clothing and hats. But this, alas, is as close as the stork gets to the dizzy peaks of haute couture, let alone the social soirées of the beautiful people.

Imagine a cantankerous 90-year-old granddad, a man who had smoked two packs a day from the age of eight and knocked back a case of brandy once a week, and you will start to form a picture of what a marabou stork looks like when it hatches from the egg. From that point on, it's straight downhill, at least in terms of appearance. Adult birds are bald, blotchy, hunched and have a floppy pink pouch hanging from their throat; throw a tatty black cloak, borrowed from a Victorian undertaker, over their shoulders, clip on a prodigious pterodactyl beak, and, *voila*, the ensemble is complete.

Not that the birds would give a bat's entrails what we think. Once upon a long time ago, some of us were lunch as far as they're concerned. Archaeological digs on the island of Flores have unearthed some evidence that ancestors of the modern marabou, over 2 meters (6.5 feet) tall and just as ugly, preyed on the miniature proto-human inhabitants. They may even have contributed to the eventual extinction of this little race of Flores hobbits, as they are endearingly if somewhat colloquially known to science.

The modern marabou hasn't shrunk much, still reaching a height of about 1.5 meters (5 feet), but modern humans have grown bigger, or at least fatter, largely thanks to our penchant for wolfing down just about every other organism on the planet. We are no longer on the menu, but

in sub-Saharan Africa, where marabous now live, they still like to keep a beady eye on us, or more particularly on our vast and ever-expanding rubbish dumps. Scavenging has always been a way of life, but the storks have not previously experienced a bonanza on this scale; the result has been a measurable increase in their numbers, at least in their East African stronghold.

Never in a good mood at the best of times, marabous living in close proximity to human settlements are known to get quite testy if the supply of edible crap dries up. The local inhabitants can expect a lot of belligerent bill clattering and muttered reminders about Flores if they toss out nothing but broken appliances, old mattresses, cracked crockery and other inedible rubbish.

Back in the pristine wild lands, marabous live a more conventional life. They often join vultures, the other baldies of the savanna, sticking their heads into the gory cavities of dead elephants and other deceased creatures. If a large animal dies of natural causes and is still intact when it keels over, marabous have to wait for the vultures to unzip the carcass, but when that's done, they lord it over all, pushing the smaller birds aside and taking what they want.

But it's not all about making do with dead stuff. These storks also hunt live creatures of manageable size, and particularly so while raising a brood of chicks. Any caring parent wants what's best for its young, and marabous are no exception. Adults may be able to swallow week-old carrion and other rotting leftovers loaded with just about every conceivable strain of ghastly bacteria, but the chicks need health food. Small rodents and reptiles, fish, frogs and the young of other birds are all items routinely added to the menu. Around the lakes of East Africa's Rift Valley, marabous occasionally cause consternation among camera-clicking tourists by preying on young flamingos, an event akin to an ogre slaughtering a dainty princess in the capricious human imagination.

Like other storks, marabous are community breeders, building large nests of sticks lined with grass, and featuring other modest creature comforts, on the top branches of flat-topped acacias and similar suitable trees. The nests are safe from the ground but vulnerable to the wide-open African sky, which is amply loaded with raptors. Having vigilant neighbors helps, but both parents need to share the 30-day incubation process, and then generally take turns to be in attendance for three to four months until the chicks have fledged.

Marabous know where babies come from, or more likely, don't give it any thought. It's safe to assume, though, that they don't subscribe to the belief that the bundles of joy are delivered in pristine napkins by their sissy white stork cousins.

AFRICAN BUFFALO

They have never met, are only distantly related, and have never exchanged so much as an email, but the African buffalo and the American bison have a great deal in common. They're big and heavy, generally placid, and they like eating plenty of grass and living in large herds. Because they tend to appear more intimidating than a domestic bull, both have lent their likeness to cheesy movies featuring the mythical Minotaur. Most folks in the USA even call their bison "buffalo," and I'm not going to risk getting letters from their lawyers by making an issue of that.

There were once over 50 million bison roaming the Great Plains of the fledgling USA, but in the early 1800s an orgy of hunting, unimaginable in scale, soon plunged their numbers rapidly down to an extremely modest 541. Trains were even laid on so that gun-happy townsfolk could happily blast away and then chug on down the track, leaving the dead and dying animals pointlessly littering the landscape. It all happened in less than a lunatic's lifetime. Bison have since recovered somewhat, and now number around 150,000, very thin on the ground by past standards, but enough to satisfy the curiosity of tourists, and salve the soul of anyone who cares.

The African buffalo had its own close shave with extinction about a century later, but the main problem was a virus, not bullets—although there were plenty of those still flying around as well. A virulent rinderpest outbreak decimated buffalo herds, along with a host of other species, in the closing years of the 19th century. The once large herds in the embryonic Kruger National Park were reduced to a handful by the time the outbreak eventually subsided. Under the watchful eye of James Stevenson-Hamilton, the first warden, numbers slowly climbed back over the next few years, although the virus waited in the wings for a periodic encore. It has only recently been totally eradicated, amid much fanfare and optimism.

It's not nice to be known for one's diseases but buffaloes bear the burden with characteristic stoicism. Included in the list of lethal ailments, which they can pass on to domestic cattle, are corridor disease, foot-and-mouth and bovine tuberculosis. When the rains come, the grass grows and times are good for buffalo, so these diseases tend to remain largely dormant; and buffalo are, in any event, all confined to game reserves these days. Nevertheless, such is the comparative rarity of disease-free buffalo that they pass between game ranchers for huge sums of money.

Happily, buffalo are probably better known for being members of the Big Five, the exclusive group of animals designated by the big-game hunters of yesteryear as the most dangerous to hunt on foot. Given the undoubted credentials of the other four, it's no mean feat to have been awarded the honor. To merit it, quite a few minor European aristocrats must have lost their pith helmets and met their maker on a buffalo's horns.

As far as is known, buffalo don't cut a notch in their horns for every human being they've killed, but if they did, the tally would probably be impressive, even today. Nevertheless, a sense of perspective needs to be maintained, and the golly-gosh lists that appear here and there should be met with caution. Domestic cattle kill a surprisingly large number of

people around the world every year, usually by accident, but then so do fudge sundaes.

When somebody isn't trying to shoot them, buffalo are generally peaceful and content. In a large herd they feel secure and, while cautious, if they see something new or unusual, they are often overcome by curiosity. They are second only to giraffe for their propensity to stand and stare, often in the middle of the road when you're in a hurry to get to the camp toilets. When they do get spooked and stampede, it's usually because they've caught a whiff of lion, the nemesis for which they reserve most of their ire and indignation.

Despite looking a bit of a shambles, a herd of buffalo is actually reasonably well organized and surprisingly democratic, at least in terms of their travel arrangements. When they move off *en masse* to find fresh pastures, they plod after two or three randomly appointed individuals, usually female, and never the dominant bull. He's usually somewhere toward the front and in the center, the safest place. Nevertheless, if they do run into a pride of lions or some other threat, the big enchilada soon comes forward to confront the aggressors, joined by other bulls. Behind them the calves and females keep to the center.

Lions pride themselves on being crafty and will do their best to isolate an individual, though the outcome is by no means certain even when they succeed. Buffalo are among the few species to demonstrate true altruism, coming to the aid of one of their fellows at considerable risk to themselves. This is especially likely to happen if the victim is a juvenile and bellowing loudly about its unfortunate predicament. Pitched battles between herds of buffalo rescuing one of their own from a pride of lions are well documented. The fact that a young victim sometimes emerges, a bit wobbly on its feet but otherwise intact, shows just how extraordinarily tough a buffalo can be.

Old buffalo, like old elephants, have dental issues, and when the time comes, they leave the herd to find a place by the river. Two or three cantankerous old codgers, who have all reached retirement age together, often hang out, enjoying the soft aquatic vegetation and rolling around in the mud to ease their creaking joints and rid themselves of parasites. Such individuals often have massive horns, a lifetime in the making, and it was inevitable that big-game hunters on their grand safaris would home in on them. The old buffalo's one advantage was that he knew all the grassy corridors and nooks and crannies of the bovine equivalent of the Shady

Acres retirement home. So even if he was wounded he could still find a way to circle round, come up behind, and toss his inept tormentor into the great hereafter. Of such stuff, legends are made.

LEOPARD

The Romans imagined a panther with a large circular spot on its back that waxed and waned with the phases of the moon. For the rest, its coat was pitch black, blending seamlessly with the night. This remarkable beast attracted its prey with the sweetness of its breath, each exhalation being so enticing as to be irresistible to other creatures.

That may sound implausible but the panther—though never a distinct species—is real enough. The name is applied to any large cat, typically a leopard or a jaguar, whose coat appears black due to an excess of melanin, the stuff that gives us our own skin color. The cat's spots and rosettes are still there, though usually only visible in bright sunlight. It seems fair to assume that a melanistic leopard, and perhaps one or two jugs of wine, contributed to the conjuring up of the Romans' fabulous lunar creature.

Leopards have no need of magic or even irresistible breath because their spotted coat plays with light and textures in the bush to render the cat practically invisible. Even when stared at from close quarters in thick undergrowth, a leopard often only resolves into startling clarity after several minutes, like the trick image in a visual puzzle. Adding to this talent, their compact size enables them to conceal themselves in places that would be an impossibly tight fit for a lion or a tiger.

Leopards are the least specialized and the most adaptable of all the big cats. Eight subspecies, differentiated by size and not much else, live in a wide range of habitats, from semi-deserts to tropical forests, on plains and in mountainous regions, extending from Southeast Asia to the tip of southern Africa. In places where the lion and the tiger have long since disappeared, the leopard manages to cling on, including close to towns and cities in Africa. Seeming ghost-like at times, they have the unnerving habit of reappearing in settled areas where they've long been deemed extinct, and occasionally popping up where they're least expected.

Ernest Hemingway's novel, *The Snows of Kilimanjaro*, opens with the mention of a frozen leopard found near the mountain summit and, although it's a work of fiction, his reference is based on fact. In 1926 a climber named Richard Reusch reported finding the frozen carcass of a leopard at approximately 5,570 meters, close to the summit of Kibo Peak, and took a photograph to prove it. He surmised that the leopard had been pursuing a goat, whose remains he also found close by. The snow line was a lot lower in those days before global warming, and pursuer and pursued were presumably caught in a sudden blizzard.

Obviously dogged determination doesn't always pay off, but one sure-fire way for a species to enhance its survival prospects is not to be too picky about what it's prepared to eat. Where available, a leopard's preferred prey is medium-sized antelope such as impala and bushbuck. An adult impala provides meals for several days and represents a good return on the considerable effort expended in stalking it, killing it and hoisting it up into a tree. Without the benefit of refrigeration, the leftovers do tend to get a bit iffy by day three or four, but leopards aren't unduly fussy about that.

In areas where large prey is not as readily available, such as the mountains of South Africa's Western Cape province, local leopards make more frequent kills and eat smaller meals, typically consisting of dassies, duikers, porcupines, rodents and birds. These leopards themselves tend to be smaller than their bushveld or forest cousins.

Of all the animals killed and eaten by leopards, a disconcerting number are plucked from the branches of our own family tree. A study in the Kruger Park suggested that up to 70 percent of baboon deaths could be

attributed to leopards, while in other areas a systematic examination of leopard scats has shown that over half of all mammal species eaten by local leopards are primates.

There is ample palaeontological evidence that leopards frequently dined on our own direct ancestors, and even today they haven't entirely struck us off the menu. The current world record for chomping humans is held by the Panar leopard, which killed and ate about 400 people in India in 1910. The runner-up, with a comparatively modest tally of 125, hailed from the same general area. Both were eventually shot by Jim Corbett, the legendary slayer of Indian man-eaters. By comparison, the two man-eating lions of Tsavo in Kenya killed about 120 railway construction workers between them.

From time to time there are still isolated instances of leopards attacking people, but along with virtually every other creature, they are now much more threatened than threatening. Uncertain numbers still live outside game reserves in Africa and Asia, avoiding contact with people rather than targeting them as prey. They are the last of the great land-based predators to be unconfined, now living, alas, by the light of a waning moon.

LAMMERGEIER

Aeschylus, esteemed poet and the originator of dramatic theater in ancient Greece, probably deserved a less farcical death, but the Fates, as he knew better than most, can be cruel. Had he used a sunshade on that sunny day in Sicily long ago, the falling tortoise might have been deflected and wouldn't have hit him on the top of his bald head and killed him.

The bird that hefted the tortoise into the sky in the first place was in all likelihood a bearded vulture, relatively common in the skies of the time, and still known for its habit of picking up tortoises, some quite substantial, and dropping them from a great height in order to smash their shell. They often choose the same rounded rock as a target, evidenced by the fact that the immediate surrounds of such anvils are littered with fragments of bone and shell. Lost in thought about his next epic, Aeschylus obviously chose the wrong moment to wander through the drop zone.

The bearded vulture, also known as the lammergeier or "lamb slayer," is not a true vulture and it doesn't routinely slay lambs, let alone poets. Despite its size and ferocious, eagle-like demeanor, it is quite a timid bird and will quickly defer to other vultures around a carcass. By and large, adult bearded vultures don't join in the bun fight around carcasses at all, and it's only adolescent birds that try their luck, albeit with a distinct lack of commitment. Rotting meat seems relatively unappealing, especially if one has to muscle through a pack of bald-headed grotesques to get at it. The bulk of the birds' diet thus consists of bone, and more especially, bone marrow. They can crack open small bones with their powerful beak; bigger ones they bash against a nearby rock or resort to the hoist-and-drop method.

A lammergeier doesn't look like other vultures. It has feathers on its head and neck and a dapper pair of feather pantaloons. It's not the kind of outfit you'd want to get all messed up with guts and gore, which perhaps helps to explain why they tend to hang back from the bloody, all-you-can-eat, pass-the-ketchup feasts that other vultures indulge in. For a bird so well dressed and fastidious, it comes as no surprise that they enjoy taking an occasional bath in shallow mountain pools, and routinely apply cosmetics. Their breast feathers are naturally white, not the rich, warm orange color that is generally evident, but they are invariably stained that way as a consequence of bathing in dust that is rich in iron oxides.

A diet of bones gets a little monotonous, of course, and on occasion lammergeiers do take live prey, notably dassies and young buck, though not in the manner of an eagle. Their typical method is to surprise a luckless victim in a precarious spot and bully it over the edge of a precipice, relying on gravity to do most of the dirty work. With impressive talons and a wingspan not far short of 3 meters (10 feet), a lammergeier is certainly capable of lifting small mammals, almost up to its own bodyweight of around 5 kilograms (11 pounds). In some cultures, the illusion of immense power gave rise to the belief that they grabbed small children and spirited them away to feed to their own chicks. In reality, accidents and sinister human interventions were the likely causes of such sad disappearances from alpine meadows.

Bearded vultures live almost exclusively in mountainous terrain, choosing inaccessible cliff ledges and crevices to build their nests. Their young are born into a vertiginous world, greeted by a vista of soaring peaks and dizzy chasms. South Africa has a small lammergeier population, resident in the Drakensberg and Maluti mountains; to the north they occur in the mountainous areas of East Africa and Ethiopia; then on to Europe and the Pyrenees and the Alps, and finally east to the Himalayas. Theirs is an inhospitable world for humankind and one that many cultures have ceded, somewhat parsimoniously, to their gods.

Taking advantage of the privacy such isolation affords, and in keeping with the drama of the landscape, bearded vultures indulge in exceptionally flamboyant mating rituals. Following a series of preliminary aerial maneuvers, a pair will lock talons and free fall for hundreds of meters (yards), a process they can exuberantly repeat a dozen times and more before alighting on the nest for a head-bobbing and foot-stamping session. The odd thing is that they are sometimes not entirely alone. Peeping Toms with powerful binoculars have observed that there are occasionally three birds present: two males and a *femme fatale*, presumably hedging her bets. Aside from such quaint deviations, the birds are thought to be monogamous.

Lammergeiers like to live on a large estate and nests are consequently widely spaced, with the nearest neighbour being many kilometers away.

They construct several nests within their home range and use a different one each year, almost certainly to stay a step ahead of the parasites that turn up uninvited, even at such exclusive and lofty addresses. A nest is built with sticks and lined with wool and other bits and pieces. Seabirds, among others, often choose cliff ledges so narrow and scary that their offspring need therapy before they can summon the will to fly. In contrast, lammergeiers place a premium on roominess and stability, choosing a leeward slope and a recess sufficiently protected from inclement weather. The chick, when it hatches, can survey the astonishing scene, which might even include Mount Everest, with equanimity.

A young bearded vulture is not born with the skills to drop bones and tortoises from the sky but rather learns from observing its parents. What is included in its birthright is the freedom to roam its own empire in the sky. One can only hope this will never be denied, in any viable future, by the insatiable needs of humankind.

GOLDEN ORB-WEB SPIDER

Little Miss Muffet, of nursery rhyme fame, could certainly be forgiven for ditching the curds and whey and making a run for it if what came and sat down beside her was a large and colorful *Nephila fenestrata.* These invertebrates look like extras from a horror movie, maybe *The Spiders That Cocooned New York.*

Miss Muffet was, incidentally, a real person, the daughter of Thomas Muffet, a 15th-century British naturalist whose keen interest in spiders was obviously a source of domestic friction. I have a particular empathy for the young lady because a similar thing once happened to me, though thankfully no curds and whey were involved.

At the time I was sitting in the back row of a game drive vehicle in Ndumo, a game park in northern KwaZulu-Natal, minding my own binoculars. As we passed under the first of a series of intimidating gigantic webs spanning the dirt track, the ranger blithely assured everyone that golden orb-web spiders were sensible creatures, and allowed ample space for large animals and vehicles to pass underneath their structures. We didn't need to duck, he said.

He was soon proved wrong, at least in respect to those of us sitting high up in the back row. As I peeled away sticky clumps of web, I noticed that a particularly large *Nephila* specimen had been dislodged and had landed on the handrail in front of me. It was casually making its way on long striped and pointed legs toward the dangling ponytail of the lady sitting in the row immediately in front of me. In such circumstances we are called upon to do the gallant thing, but instead I sat mesmerized by the ghastly possibilities. I imagined the ranger eventually glancing over his shoulder to discover that he was transporting six large cocoons, instead of a group of tourists.

In the event, the lady was made of sterner stuff than I. She saw the spider, plucked it from its perch and, with a casual remark, showed it to her husband on a dainty outstretched hand before gently dropping it into the roadside bushes.

Like virtually every other spider, orb-webs can inflict a painful bite if provoked but, as far as is known, their venom has little or no effect on humans. However, there's room for doubt because the world of spiders is full of unpredictable surprises. A vast web of over 40,000 known spider species covers the planet and every year new ones pop up, or glide into view on their silken parachutes. Golden orb-web hatchlings have been known to descend on New Zealand, which is not the usual address of their species; like little secret agents, they blow in from Australia, across the Tasman Sea.

There are only 15 known members of the *Nephilidae* family and four of them occur in southern Africa. The spider that involuntarily hitched a ride with our party in Ndumo was a *Nephila fenestrata*. An even bigger species, *Nephila komaci*, was discovered quite recently in Tembe Elephant Park, next door to Ndumo. Prior to that, the only other specimen of this species had been found weaving a web around Madagascar. It is now confirmed as being the largest of all the orb-web spiders, barely fitting onto a saucer with its legs outstretched.

Nephila are generically known as golden orb-web spiders because their huge webs shine like gold in bright sunlight. The show isn't for our benefit, of course; the pigments are intended to attract bees and other pollen-hunting insects. The spider can adjust the colors of its web as adroitly as a TV technician—a little of this, a little of that, depending upon local lighting conditions. The whole setup is designed to work for insect vision, which includes reflecting ultraviolet light, so we'll never get the full picture.

Some webs, like those in Ndumo, are colossal, spanning well over a meter (3 feet), not including the long support strands radiating out to tree branches on either side. Given the initial effort expended, *Nephilas* conduct essential running repairs as and when needed rather than always replacing the entire web if it's damaged, as other smaller species of weavers tend to do.

However, having spent so much time and energy building their mansion, *Nephilas* are also not that keen on indulging in tiresome ongoing non-essential DIY. Many webs consequently have large holes in them, which the owner still hasn't gotten around to fixing. The occasional passing giraffe must cause an absolute catastrophe, but bird damage is the main nuisance. The husks of insects are consequently placed in strategic positions on outlying strands in an effort to warn careless aviators, rather like macabre versions of the tacky decals some folk stick on sliding glass doors.

Nephila webs are strong enough to ensnare little birds or bats. Neither of these creatures constitutes normal fare for the web owner, though these spiders will happily suck the protein out of anything they can overwhelm. That includes the males of their species, which are tiny compared with the females, usually about a tenth of the size. When seen in the web—and there are invariably several males hoping for a bit of procreative action—they can easily be mistaken for infants rather than prospective partners.

Although they are no more loving, nor any less voracious, female *Nehpilas* are less prone than other species to indulge in nuptial cannibalism. It helps that the males seem to be much craftier at choosing the right moment to dash in and mate, usually when the female is eating someone else, and they sensibly approach from the opposite side of the web.

Few creatures prey on adult female *Nephilas*. In some areas, vervet monkeys are known to pluck them from their webs like bonbons, but other than that they are fairly inaccessible in their aerial apartments. The main casualties are the young, which fall prey to parasites, birds and predatory insects, notably damselflies. To counter this, *Nephilas* tend to cluster their webs together, forming a kind of web city that even the most nimble predators find intimidating.

Though *Nephilas* are usually found in bushveld environments, which are warm and fairly wet, a recent study discovered that golden orb-web spiders in general grow bigger and fatter when they manage to find their way into suburban environments. This is especially true where affluence allows for expansive gardens populated by tall trees and shrubs. At a posh address, the usual kind of parasites and predators are probably absent, while the pools of expensive artificial light attract just the right sort of bugs.

PANGOLIN

It is difficult to understand what nature was trying to achieve with the pangolin. A possible explanation is that she took a rare day off about 50 million years ago, around about the time she was working on the Carnivora—cats, dogs, bears and those sorts of animals. Maybe she left a junior assistant in charge of that part of the gene pool and he got the schematics the wrong way round.

Whatever the reason, the end result was a mammal covered in scales, with no teeth and a tongue that is rooted somewhere near its pelvis. The whole assembly was basically designed to eat ants and to curl up when threatened, looking like a hybrid between a football and giant artichoke. The really odd thing is that the design worked well, so much so that there are still seven different species of pangolin shuffling about or swinging in the trees today. If the assistant got a clip on the ear when nature returned, that ultimately proved unfair.

Of the seven extant species, four live in Africa and three in Asia. Two of the African species are mainly arboreal, have long prehensile tails and weigh less than 2.5 kilograms (5.5 pounds); they live in the equatorial forests of west and central Africa. This is also the main stomping ground of the giant pangolins, though their range also extends into parts of East Africa. The giants, as you'd expect, are 10 to 12 times heavier and firmly terrestrial. The Cape pangolin falls somewhere in the middle in terms of weight and size, and is the only species that occurs in southern Africa, though not, despite the name, as far south as the Cape. They are, after all, creatures of the tropics.

To a greater or lesser degree, all pangolins are faced with the imminent prospect of extinction. They are mercilessly hunted for their meat, particularly in Asia. The quantities of pangolin meat seized from poachers can be staggering: a single illegal cache sometimes represents the mortal remains of several thousand individual animals. As the numbers have plummeted in the wild, the price per kilo has soared, thereby further energizing poachers.

Pangolins are easy to catch because they can't bite and don't run very fast; instead they conveniently roll up into a ball when alarmed, so any fool and his friend can pick one up and pop it into a sack. Adding to the problem, pangolin scales feature prominently in the Asian and African pharmacopoeias of the absurd; dried, roasted and ground to a powder, they provide an imaginary cure for a wide variety of real ailments. An insatiable demand for their meat and scales has resulted in pangolins currently having the unwelcome distinction of being the most trafficked animal on the planet, a tragedy amplified by the fact that many folk aren't even aware that they exist.

In the normal course of events a pangolin's method of defense works well. Like a rhino's horn, the scales are made of keratin, a modified type of hair so hard that even the claws and teeth of leopards and lions are unable to penetrate. The big cats tend to roll pangolins around for a while and then lose interest, though they might not escape the encounter totally unscathed themselves. If a curled-up pangolin chooses to slide its tail to and fro while being sniffed, prodded and poked, a lion soon discovers that the edges of its scales are sharp enough to inflict nasty cuts.

When attending to its own business, a Cape pangolin plods through the bush on its stubby hind legs, nose to the ground, employing its tail and short forelegs now and again to help prevent itself from falling over. It's a design so odd and seemingly awkward that one is inclined to wonder why nature, after giving her assistant a good wallop, didn't simply screw up the sketch and start again. Any colony of ants would undoubtedly concur.

A pangolin's eyesight is poor and it locates an ant or termite nest mainly by smell. The strong claws on its forefeet then come into play, digging to reveal the network of little tunnels. It feeds rather like a child dipping a liquorice stick into a packet of sherbet, though with less mess and far greater efficiency. Its thin tongue is covered in sticky mucus and is long enough to be inserted deep into an ant tunnel; once tucked in, it is briefly wiggled about before being rapidly withdrawn, usually with dozens of ants stuck to it.

The tongue heads straight through the toothless mouth and offloads the ants or termites straight into the pangolin's muscular stomach. In essence it chews with its stomach, the muscular contractions aided in their task by the grinding together of small pebbles. These are occasionally ingested for precisely that purpose, along with the grit that adheres to its tongue

while feeding. It sounds like a perfect recipe for constant indigestion but pangolins don't seem worried by it.

With a veritable cosmos of ants and termites to choose from, pangolins are relatively fussy about which ones they choose to eat. And not all ants are simply food: like some species of bird, pangolins encourage certain types of ant to clamber all over them, even raising their scales to give the little critters better access. The formic acid exuded by the furious insects kills the parasites and mites that could otherwise make life miserable.

Life in general is, alas, rapidly becoming miserable for these inoffensive little oddities. All those millions of years ago, it would have been impossible to foresee that the chink in their armor would prove to be nature's flagship project: a modified ape with a turbo-charged brain and yet insufficient common sense.

NIGHTJAR

In medieval Europe, nightjars were known by a variety of peculiar names, but the most ludicrous was "goatsucker," derived from their supposed habit of stealing milk from the teats of goats. Drawing even deeper from the murky well of superstition, rural folk called them "corpse birds." Some still harbor the belief that they peck livestock for no apparent reason, drawing blood and thereby causing a type of distemper. When they're not doing that, they're the spooky spirits of children who died before they could be baptized.

To get a break from such codswallop, it's little wonder that European nightjars pack their bags, put on their Ray-Bans, and head south for the winter, mainly to southern Africa. On arrival they presumably renew their acquaintance with their permanently resident cousins, notably including the fiery-necked nightjar, renowned for its melodious voice. One of its calls is routinely likened to "good Lord, deliver us," perhaps a disbelieving reaction to hearing about the fanciful nonsense their European counterparts have had to put up with during their long sojourn overseas.

There are about 80 species of nightjar spread around the world and 19 species of nighthawk, close cousins resident in the Americas. All of them are crepuscular and spend the day being as inconspicuous as possible. Dove-sized and kitted out in freckled whites and motley shades of brown and gray to match grasses, leaf litter or tree bark, they're all but invisible when they're perched on a branch or nesting on the woodland floor. With their large eyes reduced to slits in the bright daylight, they have a vaguely reptilian appearance, enhanced by the fact that they're inclined to squat lengthwise on a branch, rather than adopt the traditional pert avian pose.

When inadvertently approached on its perch during the day, a nightjar remains motionless until the very last moment, relying on its camouflage to keep it from being discovered. This usually works well, so much so that more than one gardener, not expecting a large knob on a branch suddenly to spring to life and gape at him, has come close to having a heart attack.

Nightjars are widespread, though very patchy, in their distribution throughout southern Africa, with considerable overlaps between some species. They mostly favor woodlands and savannas where shade and cover are available, but some are able and willing to brave more extreme conditions. This is largely thanks to their ability to cope with wide temperature variations. On a cold winter's night in Namaqualand, a roosting freckled nightjar was recorded as having lowered its body temperature to a chilly 10 degrees centigrade (50 degrees fahrenheit) without ill effects. At the other extreme, nightjars have been observed incubating their eggs on hot sands in the blazing sun at the fringes of the Kalahari for the entire day without being cooked to a crisp. Their disproportionately enormous gape allows water to constantly evaporate from their throat without the need for panting.

Among further distinctions, nightjars are famous for being one of the very few birds to have a fine set of whiskers. These protrude below the eyes, down and forwards at the sides of the beak. More accurately, they're modified feathers rather than hair, and their purpose is not sartorial, but rather to help precisely locate insects in flight and guide them into the bird's gaping mouth. They also help protect the eyes from being damaged by the flapping wings of moths, beetles and other nocturnal airborne prey.

As expected, a nightjar's night vision is exceptional, though it's not in the same league as an owl's. They consequently hunt in the deep twilight, morning and evening, rather than in the dead of night, extending their nocturnal activities when the sky is clear and the moon close to full. Where available they take advantage of pools of artificial light, hunting insects on the periphery as they're drawn in. On occasion they'll follow an animal or a person walking through their range in the late evening, snapping up insects disturbed in their wake. This opportunistic trait can be eerily disconcerting for a nervous country traveler eager to escape the creeping night, and get to the sanctuary of accommodation.

Nightjars are monogamous, with the male evincing a strong devotion to his chosen mate, and his mate demonstrating an equally strong devotion to the prime piece of real estate that comes with the union. The birds are adamantly territorial and, during the mating season, some of the bewildering array of woops, chop-chops, chuckoos, twitters and tweets the different species make are assumed to be a way of warning others not to intrude on their patch.

A mating pair times egg laying for the week following the advent of a full moon, though not, disappointingly, for romantic reasons. The eggs are incubated for about three weeks and this foresight ensures that light conditions are optimal, weather permitting, for the birds to hunt insects when the chicks finally hatch.

All nightjars nest on the ground and the chicks are wholly dependent on dumb luck and their camouflage for survival. If a predator approaches the nest, an adult bird may try and lead it away by feigning injury, lamely suggesting itself as an alternative and more substantial lunch. They don't always do that and it doesn't always work anyway, so a high proportion of eggs and chicks fall victim to snakes, jackals, civets and all the other usual suspects. The birds sometimes compensate for the shortfall by raising two broods in a season.

Despite the inadequacies of their breeding strategy, nightjars have managed to find a unique niche for themselves in a twilight world in which avian competition is drastically reduced and insects are seldom in short supply. In this dimly lit borderland between night and day, natural perils are still numerous, but the birds at least don't have to contend with the grotesque nocturnal creations of the human imagination.

BROWN HYENA

It's not easy having a celebrity big brother, least of all one who's on intimate snarling terms with lions and leopards and pumped up to the eyeballs with testosterone. It hurts when he bosses you about at mealtimes, cackling with laughter at your long shaggy hair, and points with derision at your smart striped socks. With a big brother like that, the best plan is to avoid him like the plague and make a new life somewhere else.

Continually harassed and bullied by the super-macho spotted hyena, the brown hyena decided eons ago to do precisely this. It wandered into the desolate wastes of the Kalahari and down to the Skeleton Coast, any place where the pickings were too lean to appeal to its overbearing relative.

Perusing the brochures prior to departure, "Skeleton Coast" must have sounded quite promising to a hyena but, as is so often the case, the advertising proved to be misleading. In the vast sandy spaces skeletons are in fact few and far between and it's usually necessary to plod many kilometers before finding a decent meal. The trip to the coast would have proved a big disappointment if it weren't for the dead seals that routinely wash up from colonies on the offshore islands, and other occasional gifts from the sea.

Finding a place with adequate leftovers is essential because there's simply no escaping the fact that the brown hyena is a lousy hunter. At a little over just half the weight of a spotted hyena, it hasn't got the brawn to tackle the kind of prey its larger relative brings down. It is also a loner, seldom, if ever, joining a gang, and thus unable to rely on the numbers necessary to corner little old ladies, let alone wildebeest. Only 5 to 6 percent of the meals a brown hyena eats consists of live prey, and even then the largest item is seldom bigger than a springhare or a guinea fowl. It's not that it doesn't try; it simply lacks the speed and agility to catch animals that are equipped to escape more proficient killers.

Being a bit clumsy and slow off the mark isn't the end of the world. The brown hyena lives by the mantra that everything that lives must one day

die, and it makes a big effort to ensure that it's in a position to pay its proper respects whenever that day comes. These hyenas routinely cover huge distances each night, nose constantly sniffing the air, and can detect the molecules dispersing from a rotting corpse from several kilometers away. If a brown hyena arrives late and all the other mourners have reduced the carcass to a pile of bones, it's still able to make an adequate meal of what's left because its jaws and teeth are almost as powerful as those of its much larger spotted relative.

As bleak as the menu may sound, the brown hyena doesn't always have to make do with bin scrapings or grisly food parcels floating in from the sea. It may lack hunting skills but it's not lacking in courage and chutzpah. Frizzing itself up to look bigger, the plucky beast is sometimes prepared to throw caution to the wind and charge in on a cheetah, or even a leopard, to steal its kill. It takes a lot of guts to do that when you're by yourself and you're not renowned for your skills in the martial arts. If the hyena chooses the wrong leopard, it can sometimes prove fatal.

Despite the fact that spotted hyenas and lions have long since been locked up in game reserves, brown hyenas still choose to live mainly in the relatively arid and desolate regions of Namibia, Botswana and South Africa. Nevertheless, they are great travelers and, perhaps sensing that their ancient nemeses are now both doing time, a few are popping up in areas they might once instinctively have avoided, including what are now the rocky suburbs of Johannesburg and the peripheries of other towns. Those that do make the trip find themselves having to contend with other problems, including the traffic.

Although the majority live in den-based family groups, a high proportion of adult male brown hyenas are nomadic, holding no allegiance to a family or clan, but rather wandering wherever the mood or a promising breeze might take them. That promise might be the hint of a female in heat or the makings of a meal. Even hyenas that are part of a family group forage alone at night after they've left the den, undertaking expeditions that can last three or four days. Unlike spotted hyenas, all members of a family, including the dominant male, usually take food back to their cousins, nephews and nieces at the den. The one notable exception is the father of the cubs who is invariably long gone: in the interests of keeping the gene pool well stirred, a local female usually mates with a passing nomad rather than the dominant resident male. This worthy not only accepts the arrangement but also helps to raise all her pups as though they were his own.

All brown hyenas seem obsessed with making sure that others of their kind know who they are, where they've been and when they were there. They do this by extruding two blobs of sticky paste from a special anal gland onto a grass stem in a process known as "pasting." The larger blob is white and the smaller black, and together they contain all the necessary information for anyone who can decipher the message. A wandering brown hyena pastes a sticky note every 10 to 15 minutes. For lack of a better understanding, it's as though it gives them comfort that someone, somewhere will care, as they amble alone in the night.

Brown hyenas routinely visit the ruins of the old mining town of Kolmanskop on the Namib coast, long since given up to the desert sands by the human inhabitants. They sniff around where the garbage cans must have been, as though they think the humans have just stepped out for a day or two and will soon be back with the shopping and continue their wasteful ways. The behavior is poignantly reminiscent of the story of Grayfriars Bobby, a small Skye terrier who visited his master's grave in Edinburgh every day for 14 years, until he himself found peace.

COELACANTH

No one can accuse the coelacanth of overexerting itself. Its routine consists of snoozing all day in an undersea cave, waking when the sun sets and then lazily drifting with the ebb and flow, gobbling up any right-sized cephalopod or fish that occasionally happens by. After a less than hectic night at the office, it lugubriously paddles to the nearest cave in its home range. It has been doing that for well over 200 million years, or roughly 73 billion days and nights, weekends and public holidays included.

Scientists harboring the mad notion that human beings should fiddle with their genes to attain immortality would do well to pause and ponder this mind-numbing expanse of time. The coelacanth managed to tick off so many eons on the calendar without going bonkers through boredom because brain matter fills less than 2 percent of its brain case. The rest is fat.

The fish caught by Captain Goosen off the Chalumna River mouth near East London back in 1938, that so excited Marjorie Courtenay-Latimer and JLB Smith, was not itself 200 million years old, of course. It was not even a sprightly 65 million, which is the number of years that the coelacanth was assumed to have been extinct, given its sudden disappearance from the fossil record, along with the dinosaurs. The best guess is that the freshly deceased specimen brought ashore in East London that would so astonish the world, or at least the ichthyologists among us, was a modest 50 to 60 years old.

The coelacanth's real claim to immortality is that it has managed to live, reproduce and remain virtually the same for an awesomely long time. If you were to travel back 65 million years to an undersea canyon off the East African coast, the coelacanths you'd encounter would look, and probably behave, exactly like the ones you see today. If you then surfaced and went on land to visit our own nearest contemporaneous relative, you'd be introduced to a little shrew-like animal that ate bugs and lived in a hole in the ground.

Gearing up for the long haul means avoiding unnecessary exertion, and coelacanths are very good at that. There's no disco dancing below 50 fathoms. Their gills are small and their metabolism is slower than a watched clock. The point of snoozing in caves in the canyon wall is that they avoid having to swim against currents all day long just to stay in the same neighborhood. For a large fish, they are also exceptionally well camouflaged. Their dark metallic-blue scales have irregular off-white spots, blending perfectly with the oyster shells peppering the black basalt cave walls. Being so well hidden means they don't need to expend energy constantly fretting about predators.

Not that there's a queue of creatures eager to eat them anyway. They taste disgusting, so much so that even Comorean fishermen, unaware of their celebrity status, used to casually throw them back on the rare occasions that they actually caught one. Their flesh is exceptionally oily, containing high amounts of urea and other unpalatable compounds, and their scales constantly ooze mucus. It's little wonder that sharks wrinkle their snouts and cruise on past to the cod and calamari section of the deep-sea buffet.

Early researchers, including JLB Smith, who coined the name "Old Four Legs," thought that the coelacanth used its lobed pectoral and anterior fins to stroll along the bottom of the seabed. This suggested the possibility that, back in the day, it might have been considering ambling up and out of the sea and maybe even be taking up jogging. That sounds strenuous and totally out of character, especially for a creature accustomed to such a laid-back lifestyle in a relatively unchallenging marine environment. Putting a final damper on the theory, modern research has shown that coelacanths don't walk, or even pretend to, and are at best a side branch of the lineage that eventually gave rise to all land animals.

Being more ancient than some of the earth's rocks hasn't meant that the coelacanth is completely out of touch with modern life. It is quite adept at handling highly specialized electronic equipment. A large organ in its snout is thought to be electro-receptive, allowing it to locate and assess buried prey and help it steer around objects. Its tiny, uncomplicated brain is situated right at the back of its cranium, possibly to ensure that it doesn't interfere with the efficient working of this remarkable apparatus by actually thinking about something.

Exactly how coelacanths manage to reproduce is a puzzle for aquatic voyeurs. They give birth to live young, but there are no obvious—ahem—external bits to indicate exactly how they manage to copulate. A coelacanth's eggs are bigger than tennis balls, the largest of any known fish, qualifying the species for yet another record. With so much yolk to get through, the embryos take their own sweet time developing in the uterus, no doubt attending prenatal classes in lethargy, and only emerge after an extraordinary 13 months. That's longer than a blue whale takes to reproduce, but then again, what's the rush?

GORILLA

Gorillas still hadn't been formally introduced to polite society by 1859, the year in which Charles Darwin's *On the Origin of Species* was first published. Nobody in Europe had yet seen a live one but this minor detail didn't prevent Charles Baudelaire, the French poet, from emphatically stating his opinion about "this gigantic ape, at once so much more and less than a man... that has at times shown a human appetite for women."

Baudelaire made his remarks in reaction to a life-sized plaster sculpture created by Emmanuel Frémiet depicting a gorilla carrying off a scantily clad woman. The artist, who freely admitted that he was cashing in on "the noise being made about mankind and apes being brothers," had submitted the sculpture to the Paris Salon late in 1859 where it was indignantly rejected as being "seriously offensive to public morality." To be fair to Frémiet, nobody seemed to notice that the sculpture was clearly inscribed "*gorille femme*," implying that the woman was being kidnapped by a female gorilla for culinary rather than sexual reasons.

Baudelaire was nevertheless voicing the general view of the time, namely that the then still semi-mythical gorilla was a hairy nightmare: rapacious, ferocious and uncomfortably close to being a kind of degenerate superhuman. Even when captive lowland gorillas eventually began to appear in zoos in Europe and America, this view persisted. The classic movie *King Kong*, originally released in 1933, depicted all that an imagined gorilla should be: ridiculously huge, immensely strong and having a penchant for abducting beautiful young maidens.

Appropriately, it would take a real young maiden to spread the truth eventually. Diane Fossey disappeared into the foliage on the slopes of Rwanda's Virunga volcanoes in 1966 to study the little-known mountain gorillas in their natural habitat and in 1983 published *Gorillas in the Mist*. The bestseller, and the subsequent film of the same name, did much to dispel the myths, not least by revealing that people were killing and eating gorillas, rather than the other way around. It also turned out that Fossey had lived all those years in the forest without so much as having her bottom pinched by a male gorilla, let alone being ravished and raped by one. She was, of course, subsequently murdered by a human being, a fate that often befalls those who convey unwelcome and inconvenient truths.

Gorillas live only in the dense tropical forests that form a broad girdle across the belly of Africa, from Cameroon and Gabon, across the Congo Basin to Rwanda. Given the historic inaccessibility of much of this terrain, it is little wonder that they remained happily hidden until comparatively recent times. Small groups of *Homo sapiens* have managed to pull off the same trick in the Amazon and Borneo, remaining "uncontacted," to use current parlance, into the present century. They used to be called "lost tribes" but this implied a measure of carelessness on the part of the rest of us.

Tucked away on the slopes of extinct volcanoes, mountain gorillas were the best hidden of all. They are the biggest, blackest and hairiest, and ironically now the most endangered of the apes—a mere few hundred remain alive in the wild and none at all in zoos. Less ponderously built and more numerous, and yet still critically endangered as a result of rapid habitat destruction and poaching, are the western and eastern lowland gorillas.

Gorillas live mainly in small family groups, consisting of a dominant male who holds sway over several adult females and offspring of various ages. The silverback, as the *pater familias* is respectfully known, is more than twice the size of the females, cracking the bathroom scales at between 140 and 190 kilos (300 to 400 pounds). Family life is regulated entirely by him and the touchy subject of female emancipation never comes up. They all move when he moves, they rest when he rests, and if he decides to sleep in, so does everybody else. The upside from a female perspective is that incidents of spousal abuse are virtually non-existent and when the chips are down, the silverback will readily give up his life to defend the family.

The daily routine for a family of gorillas seems fairly humdrum, revolving mainly around eating copious amounts of vegetation, sleeping, playing with the kids and, from time to time, energetically investing in the future of the species. That may sound like the kind of life that even a stockbroker would consider giving up his Ferrari to enjoy, but the reality is more complex. Gorillas are a genetic whisper away from being us, and subject to similar emotional stresses and strains in their personal relationships. But that is the least of their current problems. Unlike all the

other creatures that we've pushed to the brink of extinction, gorillas are almost certainly aware on some cognitive level of what is happening to them, and equally aware that there's little they can do about it.

As night closes in, the troop settles down. Each gorilla above the age of four constructs its own nest, bending branches and saplings and laying down grass and leaves to make a cozy, though ephemeral, personal retreat. Only the young can sleep in the comparative safety of a tree. The adults are too heavy and instead cluster their nests around the silverback. What they dream of, Heaven only knows.

GEMSBOK

According to one dubious theory, which romantics embrace and cynics dismiss, the fabled unicorn and the oryx are actually one and the same animal. Unicorns were apparently refused a boarding pass for Noah's ark because they'd committed some unspecified transgression, but managed to survive the Flood by scrambling aboard anyway, cunningly disguised as Mr. and Mrs. Oryx. Ever since, they've been too afraid to remove their striking black-and-white masks for fear of being recognized.

If one ignores its obvious flaws, the theory could at least help explain why the oryx chooses to live far away from prying eyes, in deserts and other desolate places. Other species of antelope would find the heat intolerable, and probably die of thirst, but the gemsbok, *Oryx gazella*, like its close relation the Arabian oryx, has evolved clever ways of coping.

Staying out of the noon-day sun is a good start but in the Namib that's not always possible, so the gemsbok has installed a kind of cerebral cooling system. Its body temperature is able to rise to levels that would normally prove debilitating, if not fatal, but unlike most other animals, gemsbok pant through their nose; an extensive network of surface veins embraces the nasal breeze and then cools the arterial blood by three or four degrees before it reaches the brain. It is thus able to keep a cool head while confronting the other challenges it faces.

Ongoing water restrictions top the list. Drought is a perennial feature of their habitat and they often have to scratch up bulbs and eat wild melons and cucumbers to obtain the water they need. Grazing in the predawn also helps as the driest grasses can substantially increase their moisture content when the air cools overnight. The relatively small amounts of water they ingest this way needs to be used very efficiently, and every organ and orifice is under strict orders to conserve the stuff. Urinating is kept to a trickle and a gemsbok's droppings would barely leave a mark on blotting paper. Some claim that their lungs are so water-wise that each exhalation contains virtually no moisture at all, and a mirror held up to their mouth would not mist up.

As for all desert dwellers, water, or the lack thereof, dictates the gemsbok's entire way of life. When it rains and the grasses grow in abundance, they tend to congregate in large herds, celebratory parties of up to 300 animals; but most of the time they form small groups, usually with fewer than 12 members. These loose family groups can typically be seen plodding through the Kalahari Desert scrub, or up and over the shifting red dunes of the Namib, in a constant search for decent grazing. They usually travel in single file, a female leading and an adult bull bringing up the rear.

It is not always easy to tell who's who in such orderly queues because gemsbok look alike at a glance, the sexes differentiated by size, and the length and thickness of their horns. Adult males tend to be larger and paradoxically have slightly shorter horns, thicker toward the base. Big-game hunters of old predictably blasted away at the gemsbok with the longest horns, only to find their victim was female, an ungallant and embarrassing blunder when measured by the bizarre etiquette of that chauvinist age.

Breeding can occur at any time of the year, though spikes in the birth rate have been noted in concurrence with the immediate aftermath of plentiful rains. Courtship is a demure event, consisting of a male falling in behind any female passing through his territory that he judges to be in the mood. He politely taps her rear legs with his foreleg and if she's receptive, she stands still and all's well; if not, she tells him to keep his dirty hooves to himself and keeps on walking.

Females separate from the herd when ready to give birth and, as with many other antelope species, the newborn is left to hide alone, curled up in the grass for the first three or four quaking weeks of life. The mother returns to suckle a couple of times during the day and usually remains with her calf during the night, though she won't approach the hiding place if a predator is loitering in the vicinity. Each morning the little calf has to find a new spot, encouraged with exasperated maternal nudges and threats to pick itself up and get a move on.

At four to five weeks old the calf is introduced to the herd. It proudly displays a fine set of small horns at this first public appearance and this gave rise to the notion that gemsbok are born with horns. Even now this piece of fake news is occasionally relayed in awed tones by folk contemplating the damage the small spikes must have done to the mother's birth canal. In reality, the horns erupt and rapidly start growing soon after birth.

A gemsbok's straight or slightly curved horns are perhaps its most distinctive feature, which speaks to the dramatic coloration and elegance of the rest of the beast. Their horns can grow to enormous lengths, the measured record being 120 centimeters (47 inches). When a gemsbok stands alone atop a lofty dune, side on, with its horns perfectly aligned, it is easy to see a unicorn instead, majestically emerging from the rays of the setting sun.

HEDGEHOG

Shakespeare had a low opinion of hedgehogs. He placed them in the same category as "spotted snakes with double tongue" and other unsavory witch's assistants. It was well known back then that hedgehogs stole hens' eggs and invaded barns at night to steal milk from cows. Little wonder that, in medieval England, they were routinely exterminated or rolled in clay and then baked in the oven. Despite being obnoxious little monsters, their cooked flesh was thought to settle the stomach and cure leprosy and elephantiasis, among other diseases and ailments, thereby proving that out of an imaginary evil can emerge imaginary good.

In contrast, the Romans thought they were accomplished meteorologists, able to accurately forecast the change of seasons and predict the direction of the wind. The Chinese regarded them as sacred, while the Incas and the Eskimos didn't have any kind of opinion because hedgehogs don't naturally occur in the Americas, least of all in the frozen north.

Charles Darwin, like many before him, believed that hedgehogs rolled around under fruit trees to impale the fallen fruit on their spines so that they could transport the haul back to their nests for later consumption. He even wrote to a magazine to relate how a friend of his had seen just such a thing in Italy. However, there is no evidence that hedgehogs have a fixed address, let alone a cozy underground home with larders, lounges and libraries. They tend to sleep rough wherever daybreak finds them, snuggling under leaf litter or disappearing into a convenient hole. As for the fruit trick, if you wander around like a toothpick dispenser, things are bound to get stuck on your back; it doesn't mean you're a hoarder.

The southern African hedgehog, *Atelerix frontalis*, is typical of its kind, one of 17 extant species, five of which live on the African continent. They are all similar in size, appearance and habits. Despite the coincidental defensive strategy, they are not remotely related to porcupines, and they're not rodents; instead they share their lineage with shrews.

Ever mindful of the powerful claws and sharp teeth that lurk in the

African bush, most small nocturnal animals try not to attract attention as they go about their business. Seeming to ignore this sensible precaution, hedgehogs throw caution to the wind and can be quite noisy, often emitting little pig-like snuffles, grunts and snorts as they bustle about in the night. If danger threatens, they can of course immediately curl up into a tight prickly ball and hiss like a snake, which deters most predators, even the big cats; but there are exceptions. Giant eagle owls frequently prey on them because their large talons and scaly feet can easily cope with the spines. In any event, an owl usually glides in and strikes before the luckless hog even realizes it has a problem.

Hedgehogs used to be classified as insectivores, but in fact they're omnivorous and will eat just about anything. Earthworms and bugs form a major part of their diet, generously supplemented whenever possible with lizards and frogs, the eggs of ground-nesting birds, the infant birds themselves, assorted fungi, fallen fruits and berries, odd bits of carrion, and even, as a last resort, the discarded fast-food detritus of outdoor human feasts. Captive hedgehogs, and even some wild ones, can easily develop obesity problems; such is their predilection for tucking in to all that the edible world has to offer. They are not that big on exercise either. In the normal course of events a hedgehog ambles along at a sedate pace, but it is capable of putting on a remarkable burst of speed when the need arises, including, perhaps, on hearing a distant shout of "free burgers." They straighten their legs, rise up and beetle along like a plump Victorian matron lifting her skirts, having suddenly remembered she left some cakes in the oven.

Flippancy aside, hedgehogs have sound reasons for bulking up when food is plentiful because they're not at their best when the average temperature dips down to about 15 degrees centigrade (59 degrees fahrenheit), soon becoming dozy and uncoordinated. Although there's no evidence that they hibernate in the technical sense, they do become inactive in southern Africa and are seldom seen in the deep winter months. A hedgehog that hasn't been able to fatten itself up during the good times is unlikely to survive to see another season.

Hedgehogs are solitary animals, if not actively antisocial. When they bump into each other they let rip with indignant and cantankerous chatter and repeatedly charge, butting heads. The first one to get a headache loses. Things are different when they encounter a prospective mate, of course; on such auspicious occasions, far from becoming smooth and refined and whipping out a bunch of roses, they get even noisier. The amorous couple circle around each other, interminably sniffing and blabbering about inconsequential things that matter only to hedgehogs. With this routine complete, the female flattens the spines on her rump and the male hoists himself into position, clamping his teeth to the spines on her shoulders. The male has a remarkably long member though not one that can be regarded as disproportionate, given the circumstances.

Rather like a fakir's bed of densely packed nails, a hedgehog's spines won't penetrate skin unless significant pressure is applied, so these little creatures can easily be picked up. They are banned as pets in many jurisdictions, including South Africa, but in recent years have become popular, particularly in some states in the USA where they're locally bred, having been originally sourced mainly from East Africa. The fascination is fueled in large part by their portrayal as cuddly toys and affable or dynamic cartoon characters. Times change, but even when coddled and cuddled and dressed in doll clothes, the hedgehog, like any wild creature, remains neatly wrapped in its own enigma.

WASP

According to a legend of the Baila people of Zambia, all the earth's creatures were fed up with being perpetually cold and wet, so they decided to put together an expedition to visit the creator god in the heavens and ask for fire. The motley group of volunteers included a wasp, a fish eagle, a vulture and a crow. They duly set off together, but one by one their bones fell from the sky until only the wasp remained to soldier on. It didn't get there either. The creator god descended to meet the wasp half way, impressed with its courage and determination—and, let's be honest, worried that it would be hot, bothered and highly irritable, if and when it did finally arrive. The request for fire was quickly granted.

We may also have wasps to thank for our crockery. Many folk are convinced that potter wasps, of the family Eumenidae, gave our forebears the idea for making pots from clay. These enterprising insects use mud or sand, mixed with water and saliva, to construct their nests. Some of their vase-shaped structures, complete with a slender neck and a rounded lip, closely resemble miniature versions of the amphora the ancients used to store wine and olive oil. Quite how the ancients managed in the days before an observant Neolithic wine merchant finally woke up to what the wasps were up to is never fully explained by proponents of the theory.

There are tens of thousands of individual species of wasp, but by and large they fall into one of three major groups: the loners, the socializers and the parasites. Altogether they're a tough bunch, so much so that wasps, and their antics, shook Charles Darwin's faith in a beneficent and omnipotent God. He couldn't get his head around the notion that an insect had been deliberately created "with the express intention of feeding within the living bodies of caterpillars."

Most adult wasps are in fact vegetarians and only sip nectar, if they take time out to ingest anything at all. It is their larvae that need protein in order to grow, and eventually pupate, and the adults have devised various ingenious and—in our eyes—gruesome ways to ensure that they get it.

Social wasps tend to be the least macabre, though the term "social" refers to their nest-building activities, rather than any fondness for forming book clubs or propping up the bar at the local golf club. Included in this family are paper wasps. They construct nests using tree bark and other vegetable material, chewed into a paste and then laboriously worked into a series of cozy hexagonal cells. These are collectively attached by a fibrous stalk to a branch, a rock overhang, or in some other sheltered spot, like your front porch. Work on the nest is started by a single fertilized female, joined in due course by others. Depending upon the individual species, some of these housing developments can become quite large, though they never remotely approach the size or social complexity of a bee's nest.

Eggs are duly laid in each cell and the adult wasps then go on their grisly hunting expeditions. Like human serial killers, each different species of wasp is usually a specialist, with its own favorite target, typically a specific type of spider or caterpillar. When they find what they're looking for, they sting it to death and then dismember the corpse, chopping it up into portable portions. These are carried back and stuffed into the cells at the nest so that the larvae can get stuck in the moment they hatch. Some species apportion a set amount per cell and then put the lid on, leaving the larva to eat in private and then pupate. In others, the cells are kept open and the greedy larvae are repeatedly fed, even popping their heads out to ask for more, until they seem ready to pop. Only then does Mom turn out the lights and seal them in.

In contrast, solitary wasps don't bother about the tedious and finicky business of making egg box condominiums; these loners prefer to use the body of their prey as both a cot and a source of baby food. *Hemipepsis capensis*, a large black wasp, is a flamboyant but otherwise fairly typical representative of the type. It noisily cruises the byways of southern Africa in search of big, hairy baboon spiders. Contests between the two antagonists are dramatic, but the agile wasp invariably overcomes its large adversary, delivering a powerful sting that totally immobilizes—but doesn't kill—the hefty arachnid. The stiff, to borrow Mafia terminology, is then dragged to a suitable spot where the wasp digs a shallow grave and rolls in the body. It then lays a single egg on the spider's comfy abdomen, covers up the evidence, and departs. The spider has to wait in the dark for about 10 days, unable to even twiddle its thumbs, before the egg eventually hatches and the wasp's larva starts to eat it alive.

Grim as this is, it seems to have been the parasitic wasps that particularly gave Darwin the heebie-jeebies. They dispense with all formalities, laying their eggs directly *into* the living body of their victim. This can even include the larvae of other wasps. One species of *Ichneumon* wasp is parasitic on the wattle bagworm, thrusting her ovipositor down into the worm's body and depositing a single large egg. When it hatches, the wasp larva is able to happily move around the bagworm's roomy insides, sucking up its juices prior to eventually settling down to pupate within the dried out husk. It may sound ghastly, but parasitic wasps help to keep a wide variety of troublesome insect species in check, many of which eat our crops or decimate our plantations.

Wasps make no demands on us, other than insisting that we stay away from their nests and mind our own business when they're going about theirs. Social wasps usually give fair warning when their nest is approached, raising their wings as a signal and sending out a scout to tell any nosy parker to back off. If that doesn't work they attack without hesitation, inflicting painful stings. Unlike bees, an individual wasp can sting again and again, without damage to itself. It's little wonder that the Baila creator god didn't fancy having one angrily buzzing about his celestial apartment, maybe making him an offer he couldn't refuse.

WILDEBEEST

In the popular 1950s song, "I'm a gnu," the animal narrator has no doubts about his own unique identity, but others have struggled. Swedish naturalist Anders Sparrman, writing in 1797, placed the unusual creature between an ox and a horse, and called it a *t'Gnu*, claiming in this written word to have replicated what the Hottentots called it. In so doing he unearthed enough material for modern philologists to debate until the end of time.

Even earlier, no-nonsense Dutch explorers at the Cape had simply called it a wildebeest, because it looked a bit like a cow, or at least some sort of bovine that had not yet enjoyed the dubious benefits of domestication.

We now know that wildebeest are a type of antelope and that there are two distinct species: the black and the blue. The latter has been renamed the common wildebeest by serious naturalists because it's impossible to say "blue gnu" and keep a straight face. They're also more numerous and widespread than their smaller black cousins, and they aren't really blue. Common wildebeest are further divided into five subspecies, the most famous being the western white-bearded wildebeest, which lives in East Africa and has featured in countless wildlife TV dramas. These invariably involve a bungled river crossing and a supporting cast of gigantic crocodiles.

The black wildebeest lives in South Africa, and is the one Sparrman wrote about. It is significantly smaller, less imposing and more sedentary. By way of modest compensation, it sports a natty white tail.

The common wildebeest's odd bodily configuration evolved to meet the demands of a particular lifestyle, namely staying a step ahead of the weather and the animals that want to eat it. Locomotion experts point out that powerful forequarters, sloping down to a less muscular rear, are pretty much ideal for quadrupeds that routinely need to cover long distances at a moderately brisk and steady pace. Significantly, another animal that fits the same general body shape is the spotted hyena, one of its principal predators. Over the past million years and more, the two animals have

obviously worked out at the same gym.

The wildebeest is a living testament to the fact that the grass really is greener on the other side, at least when you take seasonal rainfall patterns into consideration. Short green grass is the stuff of life as far as these antelope are concerned; if absolutely necessary, they will make do with other items from the vegetarian platter, but their broad muzzles and dentition are specifically designed for eating lots and lots of short green grass.

The famed Serengeti migration, at which hordes of tourists link up with tens of thousands of wildebeest, is all about grass—or, in the case of most of the bipeds, getting one up on the Joneses back home. The same sort of migrations happened in southern Africa before the advent of rifles, agriculture and millions of miles of barbed-wire fencing. The last attempt at keeping to the ancient ways took place in 1983 when about 80,000 wildebeest perished in the drought-stricken Central Kalahari Game Reserve in Botswana. The old route to greener pastures was blocked by a fence.

Leading a gypsy life has called for special procreative adaptations and arrangements. These are still evident in populations that long ago had to put away the family atlas and sell their caravans. A wildebeest calf is the most precocious of all the antelope, up and about less than five minutes after birth. This is essential when everyone else in the herd has packed their bags and is agitating to get going. Another good reason to jump quickly onto the bus is that newborn wildebeest are light tan in color, more or less the same color as the infants of most other antelope species. This is great if you intend hiding out in long yellow grass for a while, as most other infant antelope do, but useless if you're born on an expansive green lawn on a featureless plain.

To make life easier, or at least less risky, female wildebeest manage to coordinate birthing so that most calves arrive within days of each other, a sudden baby boom that creates a glut for lions and hyenas. These worthies may think that all their Christmases have come at once, but what the satiated and burping predators probably don't realize is that this prey birthing strategy helps to keep their numbers down over time by ensuring leaner pickings throughout the rest of the year.

Male wildebeest also have to adjust to a life of love on the run. They still feel the need to carve out a territory, no matter how modest or temporary, but things must truly get disconcerting when every eligible female keeps glancing at her watch and muttering about being late for the next stampede. During the rutting season in the crowded Serengeti, each bull eventually has to make do with a territory the size of a postage stamp. It's not surprising that they become agitated, bellow their heads off, and resort to all kinds of over-the-top buffoonery, including bashing the shrubbery to bits.

Beating the stuffing out of struggling young trees doesn't obviously ease the path to true romance but it does have one positive spin-off: the fewer trees, the more grass. Wildebeest have, in effect, been shaping their own vast landscape for eons; it all goes to show that behind the mask of a clown, there's often much more than you think.

GECKO

A tale was told in Ancient Greece about the fate of Ascalabus, an ordinary boy who laughed at the goddess Demeter for the greedy way she gulped down a cup of water. Not impressed, she promptly turned the rude youth into a gecko, shrinking him down in size so that he wouldn't be able to bother anyone again. The cry of the gecko could be assumed to be the boy's belated apology, or more likely a colorful epithet aimed at the crotchety old deity.

Geckos are still apologizing (or swearing) to this day; they are the only species of lizard to make vocalizations more complicated than the standard serpentine hiss. The goddess Demeter must have had to deal with a lot of naughty boys in her time because there are about 1,500 species of gecko, 60 of which occur in South Africa.

One species with a lot to say is the common barking gecko, *Ptenopus garrulus*, which inhabits the sandy spaces of Namibia, Botswana and the Northern Cape, trickling down into parts of the Karoo. At sunset they poke their head out of their burrow and let rip with a repetitive sound that has been compared to two pebbles being knocked together. Whether the calls are territorial, or constitute entreaties to a potential mate, is not clearly understood. They usually shut up when dark descends but in the Kalahari nights the nattering can go on and on, helping enhance the outdoor ambience for some and making others as cross as Demeter.

Being turned into a gecko has its upsides, not the least of which is the super cool ability to walk on the ceiling. Not all species can to do this, but the common house gecko, *Hemidactylus frenatus*, has it down to a fine art. Drawing from personal experience, the only time it is likely to lose its grip is when your wife is in the bath, directly underneath. On such occasions it's important to note whether the gecko falls onto her left shoulder or the right, always assuming you can remember which of these alternatives confers good luck, at least according to the Indonesians. Dwelling too long on this seemingly irrelevant topic can, of course, generate marital strife.

Geckos are able to walk up walls and even upside down because they have adhesive pads on the toes of their splayed-out feet. That is one way of putting it, but the reality is much more complicated, partly involving tiny hairs and atomic and molecular forces, with their accompanying equations, all of which would probably have given Einstein a headache. Suffice it to say that the world we think we see and the one we actually live in are substantially different places, and this is never more evident than when you've just been turned into a gecko. Even the smooth surface of a mirror looks like Velcro.

The common house gecko is an immigrant species, originally hailing from Southeast Asia. They are such accomplished travelers that they've spread right around the globe, joining the eastern export drive by hitching rides in shipping containers. A female doesn't necessarily need to bring her mate along for the ride because she can store sperm for up to a year and happily lay fertilized eggs once she's bypassed customs and immigration. She doesn't even need to travel herself because gecko eggs have hard outer shells, unlike those of other reptiles, so they're better able to retain moisture and hence travel well, even when unaccompanied in cargo class.

Southern Africa's tropical house geckos must be nonplussed with the new arrivals, especially given that the immigrants are particularly well suited to hanging around lights and snapping up insects. They tend to be more on the ball and assertive than their shy and retiring South African cousins, chasing them out of the way and even making a meal of the native young.

Fortunately, urban living isn't for everyone and most geckos in any event prefer to stick to their own natural niche, living on rocks, in trees and even in the desert. The web-footed gecko has evolved to live only in the intimidating coastal strip of the Namib Desert, relying for the moisture it needs on the fogs that roll in from the sea. It uses its long tongue to lap up drops of condensation from stones, and even from its own body. The webbed feet have nothing to do with swimming, a rather redundant skill in the Namib, but instead enable the gecko to scamper over sand dunes without slipping or sinking in, and act like shovels when its digs a burrow. While geckos come in a wide variety of exciting and exotic colors, the web-footed can be almost translucent, its delicate spine and internal organs dimly visible.

In common with other lizards, all geckos have the ability to abruptly detach their tail in an emergency. This disconcerting self-mutilation isn't undertaken on a whim. The tail, though clearly not essential for survival, plays an important part in balancing and mating. Rapidly contracting muscles conduct the amputation at a specific "crisis point," where the joint is composed of cartilage; the wound instantly closes up, with virtually no loss of blood. The tail does eventually grow back, reinforced with cartilage rather than bone, but is never as elegantly proportionate as the original.

The point of this sacrifice is to distract predators while the gecko makes its escape, but not all attackers, notably *Homo sapiens*, are interested in eating the eerily wriggling tail. If the gecko survives the onslaught of rolled-up newspapers, shoes and other assorted missiles, it might creep back later to eat its own discarded appendage. It takes a lot of energy to grow a new tail and geckos, like most wild creatures, firmly subscribe to the "waste not, want not" school of thought, even eating their own discarded skin after molting. Ascalabus, as a former young member of our own improvident species, probably found this a particularly difficult adjustment as he began his new life by the light on the porch.

RAIN FROG

A typical frog, at least the kind you see in cartoons and children's picture books, is bright green, has an inane grin on its face, and squats on a lily leaf in the middle of a pond all day, croaking happily and shooting out its sticky tongue to zap each passing fly. Every now and again it takes an ostentatious leap into the water.

Given a bit of practice, that sounds quite straightforward, so it's a little surprising to discover that, of the thousands of species of frog in the world, the majority do nothing of the kind. Could it be that they have not read the script?

Rain frogs, judging by the rather grumpy expression on their faces, are definitely not available for such frivolities. They exhibit an aversion to ponds bordering on hydrophobia, and are so rotund that the merest ripple would be sufficient to destabilize a lily leaf and plop them into the water. If that happened, the indignant frog would immediately inflate itself like a little beach ball, and trust a passing breeze to bowl it along to the shore.

As is apparent from this, rain frogs can't swim. Without their beach-ball trick they'd sink like a stone. Their rear feet aren't webbed, but instead designed for digging holes. Each heel has a hard projection that helps it to shovel soft earth or sand up and around its body so that it can rapidly disappear backwards into the ground. Although it may sound claustrophobic, being underground certainly beats sitting on a lily leaf in the bright sunlight, exposed to everything with a beak and bad intentions.

Unlike its glamorous, albeit fictitious, Hollywood counterpart, a rain frog doesn't score high points in the looks department. If a fairy-tale princess were to kiss one, the chances are—following the mandatory puff of sparkling smoke—the resultant prince would look more like Quasimodo than Prince Charming. The frog resembles a small, round baked potato, overdone and allowed to cool, with frayed matchsticks stuck in fore and aft for arms and legs. A grouchy little face, pressed out from the potato skin, serves for a head.

Given its apparent aversion to water, it is not unreasonable for the casual reader to ask why it was named after rain in the first place. The answer is that it usually appears shortly before or immediately after rain, and especially so after heavy rain. Cautious at first, it sticks its nose out of its home in the ground and starts intermittently to whistle, squawk or cheep, depending upon which of the 13 species of southern African rain frog it is. Whatever dialect it speaks, it's tempting to speculate that the frog is moaning about the water damage done to its lounge carpet, but this is in fact their way of calling for a mate.

Male rain frogs are considerably smaller than the females, more or less in the proportion of a "new" potato to one suitable for roasts or mashed potatoes. Given this disparity in size, and the fact that the male has small arms, an amorous embrace is out of the question. The compatibility problem calls for a novel solution and this takes the form of a milky skin secretion that has similar properties to those of superglue. The small male literally sticks himself into an appropriate position on the female's lower back. The resultant bond is so strong that the happy couple cannot be pulled apart without serious damage to one, or both.

The strength of the bond is important because the weird combo then set about tandem digging their way backwards into the moistened ground. The fact that the earth is soft and moist after a downpour may help to explain why these frogs choose the onset of rain as the moment to set about such intricate and delicate activities.

A relatively modest number of eggs, somewhere between 25 and 50, are laid in a gelatinous mass about 12 centimeters (5 inches) underground. Their work complete, the male and female then separate, the unbreakable bond dissolving as miraculously as the wonder adhesive which, in gullible times past, you may have used to reattach the handle on your favorite coffee mug.

Many other species of frog lay thousands of eggs, draping them in an orgy of abundance as flamboyant necklaces across ponds and puddles. Assuming these eggs aren't immediately eaten, most of the myriad tadpoles that hatch are gobbled up by fish, dragonfly larvae, birds and other predators. Safe underground, rain frog tadpoles sensibly stay in their egg case, feeding on the jelly hampers left by moms and pops, and finally emerge, after about six weeks, as fully formed frogs.

Rain frogs don't appear every time it rains. The bulk of their calendar is taken up with subterranean activities, including snacking on termites and any other suitable subsurface insect that happens along. A good deal of their time is spent in sleep, disturbed, perhaps, by nightmares featuring lily pads and deep, dark pools of placid water.

AARDVARK

One dubious advantage of being an aardvark is that you're always at the top of any alphabetical list, which is strangely appropriate for an animal that is truly one of a kind, the sole member of the obscure mammalian order Tubulidentata. I can also tell you that aardvarks are a fossil species, though that's not something they are personally aware of or would probably give a box of ants about. When you can dig a hole 1.5 meters (5 feet) deep in about 60 seconds you don't need to worry about being called a mammalian antique.

Magicians of the Hausa people in Nigeria hold the aardvark's ability to vanish into the ground in such high esteem that they make and sell charms out of bits of it—ground-up skin, heart and nails. The aardvark would probably prefer to be less admired. The charm is worn around the neck and gives the wearer the ability to walk through walls. Gullible burglars are presumably the main customers.

The animal's physical appearance is bizarre enough to tax even the finest descriptive talents. It looks as though it's made of leftovers. In English it's known as an ant bear, even though there's nothing remotely bearish about it; while in Afrikaans the name aardvark means "earth pig," and this animal does indeed have some piggy features, including a piggy snout and relatively hairless pale skin, which is usually stained reddish-pink with dust.

But there the resemblance ends. It has a longish, hairless, tapering tail, thick at the base, a bit like that of a giant rat. While we're about it we could probably throw in a bit of sloth (heavy-duty claws), jackrabbit (huge, all-the-better-to-hear-you-with ears) and a smidgen of scaled-up shrew (long, pointy snout). It is out and about only after dark and, as there are no mirrors underground, is probably not too fussy about the fact that it's no raving beauty.

The aardvark's least endearing feature is its 30-centimeter (12 inch), fully retractable sticky tongue—the last thing ants and termites want to

see snaking around the corner of one of their tunnels. Using its spade-like claws, it can crack open a rock-hard termite mound with consummate ease to lap up breakfast, lunch and dinner. Claims have been made that an aardvark can consume 50,000 termites in a single night, though precisely how such an exact and methodical count was ever achieved is a moot point.

The furious stinging and biting counterattacks mounted by ants and termites are rendered irrelevant by the aardvark's thick skin.

The nutritious, if monotonous, diet is only varied by the occasional consumption of a mysterious type of cucumber, *Cucumis humifructus*, which fruits underground and is largely dependent on aardvarks to spread its seeds via their droppings. It chomps the fruit with a set of peg-like rootless teeth at the back of its elongated jaw. The complicated dentition of the aardvark could easily be the subject of a dentistry thesis, which, alas, has no place in a bedside book.

And nor, possibly, does sex, but since you're curious, suffice it to say that aardvarks are solitary beasts and pair only during the breeding season. The female gives birth to a single cub after a gestation period of seven months. The cub is weaned by 16 weeks and then it's straight onto the termites and cucumbers. It usually stays with the mother, sharing her burrow until the next mating season, but is fully capable of digging its own burrow after a mere six months.

Though you might live your whole life in Africa without ever laying eyes on one, aardvarks are relatively ubiquitous south of the Sahara, making a nocturnal living wherever there are ants and termites and earth to burrow into. They are the realtors of the bushveld, passing on second-hand but highly desirable subterranean homes to a variety of other animals, including wild dogs and warthogs. The main burrow can be extensive, relatively capacious and have several entrances. Like any sensible homeowner, the aardvark makes continual modifications and improvements.

Apart from Hausa magicians and other African peoples who hunt aardvarks for the pot, their main worries are lions, leopards and wild dogs. Their keen senses of smell and hearing give them warning of approaching danger, but when they are surprised out in the open, and don't have time to dig like crazy, they run a confusing zigzag course, presumably hoping that their pursuer will get dizzy and give up. If all else fails they fight back with their claws, but given the superior arsenal and lethal efficiency of their principal predators, that's usually not enough.

HONEYBEE

Bees are born from the tears of the sun, or so the Ancient Egyptians believed. This mystical insight probably has something to do with the fact that honey, the product of bees' incessant labor, is as close to liquid sunlight as it's possible to get. Bees need to visit upwards of 50,000 flowers to produce enough honey to spread on your morning toast, something to bear in mind when you're standing in the aisle of a supermarket scratching your backside and mumbling about the price.

Maybe you can do without honey, but if there weren't bees, there wouldn't be any marmalade or jam either. In fact, there wouldn't be a whole lot of other things. The best estimate is that bees pollinate about a third of all food crops consumed by human beings. Put another way, if bees vanished, so would a lot of the food you eat. And it's worth bearing in mind that domestic animals also depend to a large extent on food crops, so you could expect a big problem with your bacon and eggs as well.

Honeybees are members of the order Hymenoptera, which includes bumblebees, wasps, sawflies and ants. South Africa is home to two subspecies of honeybee, the African bee *(Apis mellifera scutellata)* and the Cape bee *(Apis mellifera capensis)*, with the latter generally confined to the fynbos of the western and southern Cape and the former covering the rest of the country. In between is a hybridization zone where strange things can happen, but more of that later.

The social life of bees has often been compared with that of human societies, in a rather garbled and half-baked attempt to make sense of how and why we organize ourselves into hierarchies, i.e. why most of us have to work our arses off from dawn to dusk while the boss gets to drive a Ferrari and play golf. For the bees themselves, such social inequalities are not a conundrum. The undisputed head of a bee colony is the queen, who secures her privileged position by secreting a special pheromone that inhibits the sexual development of workers, while simultaneously inducing in them a sense of social wellbeing.

There are three types of bee in a hive: the queen, the worker bees, which are all female, and the drones, which are all male. Drones are born from unfertilized eggs and have no stinger, pollen basket or wax glands. They tend to eat more than the workers and hence are bigger. Other than that, virtually their only purpose is to mate with queen bees. Feminist readers can take comfort from the fact that drones are usually booted out of the hive in autumn or when food runs low.

Workers—surprise, surprise—do all the work around the hive, gather food, tend the larvae and defend the colony when it's threatened. Like the queen, they can also lay unfertilized eggs, which hatch as drones. But only the queen can produce future queens, which are differentiated early on by diet. All female larvae are initially fed royal jelly, a nutrient-rich substance. Those destined to become workers—the great majority—are soon switched to a more modest diet of pollen and honey. Only the future queens are fed royal jelly throughout the larval stage.

When they're ready, the virgin queens leave the hive, heading for the bee equivalent of the red-light district, where drones hang out, and all the while they emit that magic pheromone. Mating takes place in flight, between 3 and 12 meters (10 and 40 feet) above ground. It is literally an explosive affair, occasionally audible to the human ear, and fatal for the drones. The queen mates with 7–10 individual drones, each allotted about two or three seconds. The result of this brief aerial orgy is that the queen is able to store enough sperm within her oviducts to last her for the rest of her life, during which she will selectively lay thousands of eggs and reign supreme over a new colony.

Cape bees can be distinguished from African bees by their darker abdomen and passing resemblance to an African bee queen. They also have an unusual characteristic in that workers are capable of laying both male and female eggs, so that if the queen dies, a successor can be raised to take her place. The downside of these characteristics is that if a Cape bee worker arrives in an African bee colony she is not attacked, and, uninhibited by the hive queen's pheromones, soon begins producing exact replicas of herself. The resultant social disorder ultimately leads to the collapse of the colony.

Worldwide, bees have bigger problems. In recent years a variety of factors, natural and artificial, have combined to put bees in harm's way. New parasite and virus strains are attacking hives, while the increased use of pesticides is having a serious impact on bees' health and immune systems. Compounding these problems, urban sprawl in many parts of the world has led to a marked decrease in available foraging sites, and noise and electromagnetic pollution cause considerable stress to bees, making them more susceptible to infection.

One pertinent piece of folklore tells us that if a bee flies into your house, it means that someone is coming to visit. If you kill the bee, the visitor will bring you bad news. There is no need here to belabor the ominous moral of that short story.

OCTOPUS

According to a Hawaiian creation myth, the present universe was cobbled together from the wreck of a previous cosmos. The sole survivor of that alien otherworld is the octopus. It's an easy myth to believe, especially if you're diving on the shattered remains of a sunken ship and come eyeball to eyeball with one of these creatures. Such encounters are the stuff of most folks' nightmares but are probably just as alarming for the octopus.

Octopuses (as opposed to the plural octopi, which is etymologically controversial) are solitary and retiring cephalopod molluscs that have famously devised a number of neat tricks to stay out of harm's way. The first of these is not to be seen in the first place. Unlike other cephalopods, octopuses have no internal or external hard parts, other than their parrot-like beaks, and are thus able to ooze into unbelievably tight spaces from which they can inconspicuously watch the predatory world go by.

All octopuses have specialized skin cells that are able to draw on demand from a palette of pigments—yellow, red, orange, brown or black—to color their skin to match their surroundings. Some species also have the muscular ability to change the texture of their skin and so blend in completely with lumpy rocks, knobbly seaweeds or the detritus on the sea floor. By and large, octopuses that are active in daylight hours and live in complex environments such as coral reefs have evolved these abilities to a greater degree than their sand-dwelling, nocturnal cousins. A few have attained a peak of contortionism that enables them to rearrange their bodies to resemble something nastier than they are, such as a lion fish or a sea snake.

When it is discovered and targeted by a predator, typically a moray eel, a shark or an agent of the Yamomoto Calamari Canning Company, the octopus rummages around in its remaining bag of tricks. First off, it releases a cloud of ink, which isn't really ink at all, being mainly composed of melanin—the same stuff that gives us our hair and skin color and protects the skin from sun damage—so you could say it's more akin to suntan lotion. It also contains a substance that inhibits the enemy's sense of smell. In some instances the ink cloud is thought to act as a pseudomorph, a bit like a matador's cloak, providing an alternative target for the puzzled predator. Hidden behind all this commotion, the octopus takes off like a rocket by pumping a jet of water through its mantle.

In extremis, and when all else fails, some species have a final trick up one of their eight sleeves. Like some lizards, they can deftly detach an arm, a relatively innocuous sacrifice, given that the arm soon grows back, no harm done.

Life for the octopus is not just about avoiding being something else's lunch. Octopuses are highly effective predators themselves. There are about 300 species of octopus and all of them, to a lesser rather than a greater degree, are venomous. The one you most want to avoid upsetting, especially if you hail from Down Under, is the blue-ringed octopus, the only one known to be lethal to humans. A tiny 25-gram (1 ounce) blue ring has enough tetrodotoxin to paralyze the entire Australian cricket team, so if you're a mollusc or a small fish your chances of surviving the innings are not very promising.

Octopus venom is delivered via their saliva and is employed to subdue prey so that it can be conveniently chopped up into manageable portions by the beak. The octopus's staple diet consists of crabs, crayfish and molluscs, though larger specimens extend their menu to include fish, even small sharks, and, if the opportunity arises, an occasional inattentive seabird.

Despite the best efforts of Hollywood, there is no plausible evidence that octopuses drag down ships to snack on the hapless crew. It would be no mean feat, given that the average common octopus (rather unfairly described as *Octopus vulgaris*) weighs in at a modest 3–10 kilograms (7-22 pounds) and spans 30–91 centimeters (12-36 inches) with its arms out. The exception is the giant Pacific octopus, which holds the record with an arm span of 9 meters (29.5 feet) and an impressive weight of 272 kilograms (600 pounds). By contrast, the largest squid so far recorded had a span of 14 meters (46 feet) and weighed more than you want to imagine.

Octopuses are more into brain than brawn. There is little doubt that they are intelligent. Why this should be so is something of a puzzle, given that their cephalopod relatives have the intellectual capacity of a jam sandwich. We humans are fond of bragging about how our opposable thumbs have helped make us marginally brighter than a chimpanzee. That may be so, but it is interesting to note that an octopus can grasp and manipulate an object with each individual sucker—and it has hundreds of them. And while we are social creatures and have the benefit of learning from each other, the octopus is solitary and learns entirely alone.

There are well-documented cases of octopuses using and playing with objects and even solving relatively complex problems, and then remembering how they did it. One enterprising individual climbed out of his aquarium tank during the night to eat the fish in an adjacent tank and then clambered home before dawn. It was some time before puzzled aquarium staff worked out what was going on, and then only because they caught him in the act.

Sex for the octopus is a terminal affair. The male dies within a few weeks of mating, and the female doesn't eat while she is looking after her eggs and then dies of starvation soon after the eggs hatch. On average, octopuses live only for about two years. Perhaps in some strange way having a brief life is the enigmatic creature's way of acknowledging the limited capacity of the earth to sustain life. Maybe the Hawaiians are right, and the octopus really does know what happened to the last world.

DASSIE

If you happen to be introduced to a dassie at a cocktail party, within minutes you'll almost certainly be told that it's closely related to the elephant. You'll hear that the family connection goes back millions of years. It's a humbling bit of information, especially when all you can come up with in the way of distinguished relatives is your Great-Uncle Bob who did quite well in the furniture trade back in the 1960s.

The dassie, or rock hyrax as it might prefer to be formally known, doesn't look like an elephant, walk like an elephant or trumpet like an elephant, and of course it isn't an elephant, but it can indeed claim to be a distant relation. When you're a small animal, and most people simply assume that you're a kind of fat rat, that's important.

If you're inclined to take such ancestral bragging with a pinch of salt, pause to consider a few common features. The tusks for a start: most mammalian tusks develop from the canine teeth, but in both dassies and elephants they developed from the incisors, albeit rather more modestly in the case of the dassie. And the feet: both have flattened nails on their digits, unlike the curved claws of other mammals, always excepting a curved grooming claw on the inner toe of the rear feet of the dassie. The elephant doesn't need one of those, having a trunk to do the job. There are also marked similarities down in the reproductive and mammary departments, though not things we talk too loudly about in polite company.

Sadly though, family connections are not always helpful. While the elephant gets to lord it over all, pushing over trees and the occasional tourist minibus and frequently getting its picture into the glossy magazines, the dassie is forced by circumstances to make a modest living in the rocks. It doesn't dig burrows, heaven forbid, rather making intelligent use of the crevices nature haphazardly creates as she disassembles the landscape. Fortunately, that happens a lot, and so the dassie is able to find a home pretty much anywhere in the country.

Dassies are well adapted to their rocky habitat: the padded soles on their sweaty feet act a bit like suction cups, enabling them to walk all over the place, even up the walls. They choose their homes wisely and usually don't have to wander very far to find something to eat. Their diet consists mostly of grass and shrubs, including some that are toxic to other species. When they perceive a threat, such as a lurking caracal or an eagle circling overhead, they can quickly scoot across the patio into the nearest crevice.

They are never at their best in the morning, mainly because they don't have a fixed body temperature. While this adaptation enables them to tolerate a wide range of climatic conditions, it does mean that they're grouchy first thing, would probably kill for a decent cup of coffee and don't want to talk to anyone until they've warmed up in the sun.

When they do get going they chatter quite happily, having at least 21 different sounds, only a couple of which have been translated. A squeal means "on your marks," and a bark means "run like hell." For all we know, the rest of it might include various insults about stuck-up elephants and moans about the injustice of it all.

A family group consists of a dominant male who holds sway over a harem of as many as 15 females, plus assorted youngsters of both sexes. Other mature males live on the periphery or have to set off to find their own digs. This can be a dangerous journey. There are plenty of shady neighborhood characters with big teeth and talons loitering about, and the dassie is very vulnerable out in the open.

Not that they're always pushovers. Despite their superficially fluffy, toy-store appearance they can be very aggressive, especially when their honor is at stake. "Australian Tourist in Hospital After Dassie Bites Off Half Her Face," screamed one recent newspaper headline in the finest tradition of over-the-top reporting. It turns out that the dassie bit her nose when she tried to cuddle up for a selfie, but it does go to show it's not wise to take liberties with one of God's own. Battles for dominance between males can get very intense, so much so that the combatants tend to throw caution to the wind and hence become vulnerable to predators.

While a local population may increase quite rapidly under ideal conditions, dassies do not breed like rabbits, at least not in the colloquial sense of that phrase. Females usually give birth to two or three cubs after a seven-month gestation period. The newborns are very precocious and start eating solids within the first few days, though they are not fully weaned for three or four months. I probably shouldn't tell you this, but eating solids includes snacking on pellets from the parental toilet, as a means to acquire bacteria essential for their digestive systems. It's doubtless a touchy subject and maybe something best kept to ourselves.

HONEY BADGER

One good thing about honey badgers is that they're not a whole lot bigger, at least if you believe the stories. The bush would be a worrisome place, even if you were a bull elephant.

Folklore is full of tales about the diminutive honey badger bringing down buffalo and other seemingly impossible adversaries—not as prey, but because the animal in question commits some real or imagined provocation. Badgers purportedly have the unnerving habit of honing in on a larger animal's private parts, inflicting injuries bad enough to cause the target of their wrath to bleed to death. No less a personage than James Stevenson-Hamilton, the first warden of the Kruger National Park, reported being a witness to such attacks on wildebeest and waterbuck. They probably don't make crotch guards in jumbo size but if I were a bull elephant I'd maybe go shopping.

Fortunately, the honey badger is a small mammal, weighing in at an average of only 12 kilograms (26 pounds). Badgers have a relatively long lifespan, about 24 years, and females have a relatively long gestation period, around six months. They usually give birth between October and January, producing two cubs. Juvenile honey badgers look just like Mom and Dad and so, oddly, do cheetah cubs. As a nod to the badger's ferocious reputation, juvenile cheetahs have evolved a similar coloration and hairy profile, only adopting the real cheetah look once they've learned to run like the clappers. Obviously Mother Nature is convinced that at least some of the stories about the badger are true.

As you'd expect from such a resourceful animal, the honey badger is widely distributed in South Africa, and adapted to most habitats except mountainous forests and deserts. It is usually solitary and is supposed to be nocturnal, though it doesn't always take much notice of that limitation.

Already a film star, the little beast is now also a YouTube sensation, and with good reason. Various film clips show the diminutive hard case facing down a pride of inquisitive lions, lunching on a big poisonous snake and—to prove it has brains as well as brawn—showing off its Houdini skills by easily escaping from cages and enclosures with a nonchalance that embarrasses its human keepers.

Not for nothing did the South African army name one of its most heavily armored machines the "Ratel," the honey badger's name in Afrikaans. Tall tales aside, when it comes to rumbles in the jungle, the badger punches way above its weight and more often than not sees off the opposition. A thick, loose hide enables it to take as much punishment as it dishes out, and it is not above emitting a disgusting anal secretion that even the malodorous hyena finds repugnant.

They may not be cuddly, but, let's face it, badgers are cute, and they have a sweet tooth. Honey is a favorite food, though not a staple of their diet. Their fondness for the sweet stuff brings to mind Winnie-the-Pooh, the much-loved, bumbling and amiable hero of A.A. Milne's children's stories. But an obsession with honey is about the only thing the two have in common. The honey badger also eats bee larvae, grubs, scorpions, spiders, birds, snakes, mice and reptiles, to name but a few items on its omnivorous menu. Given the chance, it would probably eat Pooh's tiny friend Piglet rather than have a philosophical conversation with him, and is anything but bumbling while it goes about its daily chores.

As befits its celebrity status, the honey badger occasionally has its own entourage of star-struck hangers-on, including the pale chanting goshawk and the black-backed jackal. In reality—the same reality that usually applies to the groupies clustered around Hollywood's best and brightest—their presence is not so much a case of adulation as perceived opportunity. The badger may be tough, but it is not that agile. When it digs for small

rodents, some invariably manage to dash past, their frantic bid for freedom ending abruptly in the jaws or beaks of a member of the highly attentive and nimble audience.

Perhaps the badger's most celebrated and dubious relationship is with the greater honeyguide, a small, inconspicuous bird that science emphatically labels *Indicator indicator,* just in case you missed it the first time. The honeyguide is good at finding beehives but lacks the muscle and chutzpah to exploit the discovery. Enter the hero. The bird sends a tweet to a honey badger ambling about in the vicinity and once it has its attention leads it unerringly to the hive. Given the badger's messy eating habits it's a win-win situation.

Strange things happen in the African bush, but more often than not the badger follows its own agenda and minds its own business. It is not the demon it's sometimes made out to be, but then again, would you make fun of Bruce Willis in a *Die-Hard* mood?

HIPPO

One of the most popular small statues kept in homes in Ancient Egypt had the head of a hippo, enormous breasts and the stomach of a pregnant woman. The deity's name was Tawaret, and it was believed that she protected pregnant women, mothers and small children. Paradoxically, Tawaret was the consort of Set the Destroyer, the Egyptian god of death and evil, an intimidating figure whose gloomy image seldom joined his wife's on the domestic mantelpiece.

The Ancient Egyptians shared the River Nile and its banks with hippos, and this brief glimpse into their complicated cosmology shows that they had a good understanding of the dichotomous nature of their bulky neighbors.

Hippos make exemplary mothers, but they are also credited with killing and maiming more human beings in Africa than any other animal. The reason is not that hard to find. No other large wild animal in modern times habitually lives in such close proximity to human settlements. Human beings, like hippos, need water in rivers, dams or lakes to survive, and most attacks occur on or near the water's edge in poor rural communities that don't have access to piped water. Attacks, most of which take place at night while hippos are out grazing, seldom seem to be provoked, though the highly territorial hippo probably has a different take on this.

Hippo attacks in Africa are often met with a fatalism that doesn't accompany attacks by other wild animals such as snakes, lions and elephants. "Villagers defend crime-fighting hippo" bellowed the headline of a South African newspaper in 2002. It reported that a young man rolling home at night from a soccer match had been attacked and severely injured by a hippo. Conservation officials considered shooting the offender, but the local chief would have none of that. He insisted that the hippo be relocated, a sentiment vociferously echoed by other villagers. They pointed out that the presence of hippos patrolling the environs of the village each night kept burglars and muggers at bay.

Other wild animals are often viewed as intruders, but the hippo seems to be regarded as a cranky neighbor, the type who grumpily nods hello across the garden fence, but woe betide you if you set foot on his newly mowed lawn.

Hippos are very good at mowing lawns. The vast bulk of their diet is grass, and, if necessary, they will travel a long way to find it—20 kilometers (12.5 miles) and more being an unexceptional nightly excursion. Where possible though, they stay close to their home stretch of water, be it a river or dam, nocturnally munching along the banks to a distance of 2 or 3 kilometers (1 or 2 miles) and cropping the grass with their big lips to create lawns that the Palm Beach Country Club would be proud of.

A typical hippo day resembles one that most of us dream about while we're stuck in traffic on a Monday morning: water, beach and piña coladas. In consequence they have a reputation for indolence, reinforced by the fact that every single one of them looks like a prime candidate for a Weight Watchers course. It's unfair of course; life for a hippo is far from an endless round of water sports, pigging out and snoozing.

Hippo bulls lead a particularly dangerous lifestyle, routinely suffering ghastly injuries and even losing their lives in regular battles to secure or defend their watery domain and harem, two of life's chores that routinely go hand in hand. Young males are driven away by the dominant bull when they reach five or six years old, and it is no easy thing to find alternative accommodation, especially when there are equally cantankerous and belligerent neighbors upstream and downstream.

Making it out of infancy is a perilous journey in itself. Pregnant females leave the herd to find a secluded spot when ready to give birth, but a mere two weeks later it's time to introduce junior to his plump cousins, uncles and aunts and, of course, the big enchilada himself. If after the first sniff the dominant bull suspects infidelity, or maybe just because he's in one of his moods, he will attack the baby. If this occurs the mother justifies her reputation among the Egyptians as Tawaret, aggressively keeping the male at bay, often supported in her unequal task by other females. Even if dad does give his nod of approval, it isn't all beer and skittles for the cute young butterball. Crocodiles and lions are an ever-present menace.

Despite their bursts of ferocity and the impressive human body count they manage to rack up each year, hippos generally have a benign and cuddly reputation, at least from the safe perspective of city dwellers. The legendary wanderer, Huberta the Hippo, subject of many a gooey children's story, helped in the creation of this sentimental perspective. Starting out as

Hubert until she flashed her eyelashes and showed a bit of shapely thigh, Huberta made an epic journey down the east coast of South Africa from Lake St. Lucia to the vicinity of King William's Town. She moved from pool to pool and river to river, taking four years over the trip, never hurting or threatening anyone. In the process she became a darling of the press, and there was much despairing beating of editors' chests when she met her end in the Keiskamma River, shot by hunters unaware of her celebrity status.

More recently, video footage of a hippo rescuing an impala from the jaws of a crocodile, nuzzling the hapless, half-dead creature and seemingly trying to help it to its feet, has helped reinforce the hippo's benevolent image. Other, similar rescues have been recorded and zoologists have yet to come up with a plausible explanation.

Perhaps the Great Spirit knows. African legend at least has a theory to explain why hippos disperse their droppings both in the water and on land by vigorously wagging their stubby tails. In the beginning, the Great Spirit allowed hippos to live both on land and in the water, but he was worried that with their cavernous mouths and huge appetites they would soon eat all the fish. He therefore extracted a promise that they would eat only grass and, to ensure they complied, commanded that they scatter their dung so that he could see at a glance if it contained fish bones.

The Romans gave the hippopotamus its name, which in Latin means "river horse," a description adopted from the Ancient Greeks. In Afrikaans it is known as a *seekoei*, which translates as "sea cow." Both names bestow an improbable domesticity on a creature that, in the wrong set of circumstances, can bite a person in half.

KLIPSPRINGER

If the last 200 million years have taught us anything, it's that extreme specialization is a risky strategy. Creatures that didn't want to listen have gone the way of the dodo, a bird that started out as a pigeon on a holiday to Mauritius and ended up as a kind of flightless Billy Bunter[2] with a silly beak. If it had stayed a pigeon it might have avoided meeting its demise in common sailors' cooking pots and, ironically, could even now be perched instead on Admiral Nelson's head in Trafalgar Square, attending to its private business.

The diminutive klipspringer has also failed to heed the lesson, but, remarkably, its strategy seems to have paid off, at least for the time being. Africa's vast spaces are littered with rocky outcrops, islands of a sort in an enormous sea of woodland, scrub and savanna. By a lucky happenstance many such outcrops are located in game reserves, and the small antelope cling tenaciously to them like life rafts. Barring bush fires, a pair of klipspringers might spend their entire lives on the same pile of boulders, a finite world usually encompassing a mere 20 to 30 hectares (50-75 acres), and sometimes a lot less.

Adapting to a life on the rocks has meant making major changes, beginning with the hooves. Klipspringers stand on the hard tips of their rounded hooves, which have undergone a complicated transformation and are unlike those of any other antelope. This radical adaptation enables them to get a sure purchase. Helped along by powerful hindquarters, they can effortlessly outrun, outjump and outmaneuver virtually any predator in their rocky home range. On the earth and soft sands in between outcrops, such specialized hooves are not, of course, such a hot innovation, which helps explain why the animals are committed homebodies.

Even the most accomplished acrobats sometimes slip and fall, which is

---

2 Billy Bunter featured in a British comic strip; one of his dominant
   characteristics was his large, rather rotund body.

something you really don't want to do on granite rocks. The klipspringer has taken the necessary precautions, evolving a thick, springy coat made up of hollow, coarse hair that helps cushion the impact if it gets too cocky and takes a rare tumble. An added bonus is that the coat provides effective insulation when the cold winter wind whistles through the klipspringer's craggy home.

Unlike other antelope, with their complicated harems and all the bickering and social upheaval that this inevitably entails, klipspringers are monogamous. Once hitched, they stay together for life and, in a seemingly touching display of mutual devotion, rarely stray more than a few dozen meters (yards) from each other. Only the worst kind of cynic would suggest that if you're stuck on a rock in the middle of nowhere there really aren't many other places to be.

They take turns feeding and keeping watch, occasionally taking time out to mark their territory by inserting the tip of a twig into a prominent scent gland beside their eyes. The female goes first, and the male follows, dabbing the same twig with a sticky potion and licking it to release the aroma as if in affirmation of their undying bond.

The male further displays his gallantry by taking less time eating and longer spells on watch, and especially so when junior comes along. Raising young is an anxious time for klipspringers and no picnic for the infant, which spends the first three months of its life lying flat in a sheltered crevice, hiding from raptors and other potential dangers. The young are weaned at about four months and usually leave home after a year. There is some debate as to whether they are forced out or can't wait to get away from parental control. As in our own case, both probably happen. Female offspring are more likely to remain for a while, amid scandalous rumors of incest.

Secure on the top of a favorite boulder and supremely confident in their rock-bounding abilities, a klipspringer pair sometimes likes to thumb their noses at approaching predators. When they spot a threat, typically a leopard or a hyena, both male and female stand their ground and remain in view, giving a short cry that has been likened to the blast from a toy trumpet. This lets the predator know that it's been spotted and, with the element of surprise gone, saves everyone a lot of unnecessary effort. Klipspringers tended to be easy targets for hunters with rifles precisely because of this behavior, and in the hunt-happy days of yore many ended up donating their well-cushioned coats to be used as saddle stuffing.

When all is said and done, perhaps the klipspringer has its own lesson to impart after all: if you find your perfect niche, maybe it's best to stick with it. Kicking off your shoes or throwing your flight feathers to the four corners of the wind on an idyllic tropical island may seem a good idea, but you can never really know who or what may one day come sailing up over the horizon.

SPOTTED HYENA

If, by some bizarre quirk of fate, you found yourself acting as a public relations consultant for a pack of hyenas, it would be best to insist on payment in advance; yes, payment in advance, maybe a tooth-proof vest and a guaranteed place in the witness protection program.

Spotted hyenas have never made much of an effort to get along with anyone, even each other. The word "popular" doesn't feature in their lexicon, and they don't seem to give a hoot about their image, often cackling with hysterical laughter when some other animal takes a tumble and gets dismembered in the bush.

Big-game hunters in the first half of the 20th century regarded them as barely worth a bullet. They were cowardly, shifty reprobates who made a living by butchering the sick and helpless and scavenging rotten leftovers. They could always be found hanging around the tables of other noble and bullet-worthy carnivores, typically lions and leopards, or otherwise outside a safari tent looking for an opportunity to steal stuff.

The first dent in their implacably evil reputation was made in Tanzania's Ngorongoro Crater in the 1970s. Research revealed that hyenas surrounding a pride of lions as they dined imperiously on a zebra carcass might not be the riffraff we'd always supposed. It turned out that more often than not, at least in the Ngorongoro, the carcass belonged to the hyenas—they had hunted and killed the hapless zebra during the night. The lions were the robbers and then had the gall to put on a breakfast show for camera-wielding tourists. All those happy snaps were taken under false pretenses.

If hyenas are aware of this cautious and subtle shift in public opinion they don't seem to have taken much notice, presumably because the revelation is nothing new as far as they're concerned. They still live their nocturnal lives, doing the nefarious things they've always done. That includes eating people when the opportunity presents itself. The corpse-strewn battlefields in the horn of Africa have lately provided a bonanza for spotted hyenas, so much so that they are now taking more of an interest in live bipedal specimens. In Malawi, they have a long record of chomping humans, particularly during the hot season when it's cooler to sleep outside. In the rest of rural Africa such incidents are almost certainly underreported.

The fact that hyenas don't get the same publicity as other man-eaters is probably because we don't like to admit to the idea. It's one thing being gobbled by an awesome great white shark or chewed by the king of beasts, but a skulking, cowardly hyena? Another reason, to be fair, is that killing human beings is not something hyenas really do that often. If you choose to believe everything else about them, the one thing worth admitting is that their risk-assessment skills are second to none. Killing and eating humans who have access to guns and tend to form outraged mobs is a decidedly risky business.

Hyenas evolved, at least in part, to cash in on the fact that the other major predators are wasteful eaters. A lion typically consumes only about 60 percent of a carcass, leaving plenty of marrow-filled bones and other bits and pieces. Hyenas' jaws and titanium teeth are able to exert immense pressure, enough to crack open and break apart even the largest bones. That done, their digestive juices are so potent that they can efficiently process virtually any organic matter, including bones, hooves, hides and even horns, thereby extracting the last ounce of nourishment from even the bleakest pile of animal remains. They're not bothered about medals, but cleaning up the landscape should at least earn them some brownie points with the environmental lobby.

The benefit of eating things that are dead already is that you don't have to risk life and limb tackling something that might fight back. Even the most innocuous-looking quadruped can sometimes land a devastating kick or may stick its horns into all the wrong places. Nor do you have to expend energy chasing after fleet-footed meals. Unless it's absolutely necessary, you can leave that to the glitzy superstars. When they've done what's required it's just a matter of hanging around or, in the case of leopards, scaring them up a tree and waiting for bits to fall. With any luck, the whole carcass drops in your lap. When it comes to stealing kills, cheetahs are a bit of a joke as far as hyenas are concerned. Unfortunately there aren't that many of them, and sometimes, like it or not, you just have to do your own dirty work and hope that the local lions don't switch roles with you.

To the casual observer the social life of spotted hyenas is something of a

shambles. It's not always clear who's who, who belongs to which gang, whether there even is a gang, or if they're just a lot of layabouts with shifting mutual interests. They can be found alone or in packs of anything up to 60 or 70 individuals. Even a communal hunt doesn't seem to be pre-planned but rather a question of joining in on an individual initiative.

Female hyenas are big, butch and scary as far as the browbeaten males are concerned. Even an adolescent female can see off all but the largest and most dominant males. They are pumped up with so much testosterone that confusing things have happened to the female genitalia, which, at a glance, look just like a male's you-know-what. As a result, for a long while hyenas were thought to be hermaphroditic, yet another thing to add to their weirdo image.

Hyena cubs are born in an underground den with fully functioning canines that they invariably put to good use dispatching siblings of the same sex, the only mammal known to do this. Mothers usually give birth to twins, so if you pop out as a male you have to keep your paws crossed that you have a sister not a brother, or vice versa. The statistical result is that about 25 percent of hyena pups never get to see the light of day.

If you set out to create an image as the most obnoxious kid on the block, you couldn't do a better job than the hyena, nature's newest type of carnivore. But then again, who will blame us for trying? As we bomb, shoot and rapaciously consume our way toward extinction, they may yet have the last laugh.

SECRETARYBIRD

Among its many other esoteric distinctions, the secretarybird is a favorite of postal authorities around the world and has featured on more stamps than most other birds. It has pride of place in the coat of arms of South Africa and is the national symbol of Sudan. Its image is also used in the logo of the Malaysian Association of the Institute of Chartered Secretaries and Administrators, symbolizing professionalism and high moral standards. Although the secretarybird is totally absent from Asia, this honor is presumably inspired by the bird's reputation for never cooking the books and going straight home to its mate each night.

The secretarybird purportedly got its strange name because the black feathers sticking out of the back of its head reminded Victorian observers of office clerks, who would habitually put quill pens behind their ears when turning the pages of their ponderous ledgers. Another and more plausible theory suggests that the name actually derives from an Arabic word meaning "hunter bird," which sounds very similar to the French *secretaire*. Whatever the origin, we're stuck with it. Given a choice, and assuming it mattered, the bird would probably prefer to be known by its other, less used but more accurate colloquial name: the marching eagle.

Although assigned to its own distinct family, *Sagittarius serpentarius* is in effect an eagle on stilts, replete with beak and talons. It is superbly adapted for a life on the open veld and can surely be thankful, despite the name, that it's not stuck in a stuffy office with a boss continually making inappropriate remarks and trying to ruffle its feathers. Its association with serpents derives from the fact that when it finds a snake it stamps the stuffing out of it, its feet and claws exerting a force that could break your hand. This dramatic routine earned it the respect of many snake-fearing African communities and in consequence it was largely left alone.

Depending upon their availability, snakes usually form a relatively small part of the bird's diet, though the secretarybird will always enjoy them when it can—fat or thin, big or small. It swallows small snakes whole, but larger specimens are torn to pieces with the bill. Although well protected by its feathers, it's not immune to snake venom and takes due care to ensure that the object of its merciless stamping is well and truly dead before feeding. On rare occasions this entails hoisting the snake into the air and dropping it from a great height, a method employed by bearded vultures to crack tortoise shells. On a humdrum day the bird selects from a standard menu that includes insects, lizards, mice, chameleons, locusts and other invertebrates. There have been reported cases of secretarybirds preying on cheetah cubs and other infant mammals when the opportunity presents itself.

The birds are endemic to Africa, living on open grasslands from the fringes of the Sahara Desert to the Cape of Good Hope, as far away from an office as possible. Given their lifestyle they shun forests, thickly wooded areas and mountainous regions. In keeping with their black-and-gray air of official gravitas they are largely silent, occasionally uttering a guttural croak.

The birds are committed to a terrestrial lifestyle, covering several kilometers a day at a steady pace. They pause every now and again to stamp on the ground, wings outstretched, to cause a local commotion and flush out the edible inhabitants of the long grass. When threatened itself, the secretarybird runs at first, often with partially opened wings; only if that's not enough to elude a determined pursuer does it finally take to the air. These birds can fly very well, resembling storks rather than eagles in flight, and have been observed riding thermals to heights of 3,000 meters (10,000 feet) and more. To keep fit, or more probably to advertise their presence to others of their species, they fly around their territory before settling down for the night.

True to their imagined Victorian values, male and female often keep a respectable distance from each other while they're out walking in the veld and thus often appear to be alone. By contrast, their mating displays throw decorum to the wind and are exceptionally flamboyant. Male and female soar in wide circles, swoop and plunge toward earth, sometimes clasping each other's talons like two mutually besotted skydivers.

The birds generally pair for life and build a nest together near the top of a tree, preferring the flat top of an acacia, but making do with other types of tree or even a tall bush where necessary. The important thing is that the nest be impregnable from below, which it invariably is, and hence very difficult to spot from the ground. The flip side is that it's visible from the air, and the chicks are sometimes targeted by other raptors if both parents are absent. The birds are remarkably faithful to their nest, returning to roost at night even when no eggs or chicks are present. The flat bundle of sticks grows year by year in the manner of an eagle's aerie and can eventually expand to a diameter of nearly 3 meters (10 feet)— more commodious than the average office cubicle.

A female lays two, and often three, eggs. They hatch at short intervals, as incubation begins with the first egg. A consequence of this is that the last chick to see daylight usually dies of starvation, being unable to compete with its slightly larger siblings. The young birds can fly after about 80 days, but they often leave the nest to strut their stuff a few days before they're able to take to the air. When that day finally comes, the young birds clear their desks and leave the building, living a nomadic existence until, hopefully, they find a mate

.

AFRICAN CLAWLESS OTTER

If you drop dead and it turns out you have to be reincarnated, maybe choose to come back as an otter, especially if you enjoy water sports, fish and crustaceans. Of all the animals struggling to get some modest pleasure out of life, including us dumb nuts, otters seem to have it made. They are top of the food chain in their semi-aquatic wonderworld, and can eat 15 percent of their body weight every day and still keep fit and trim—you try tucking in to 6 or 7 kilograms (13-16 pounds) of your favorite foods and see what happens.

What's more, they are so well adapted to their eco-niche that they don't have to spend the whole damned day at the office trying to put food on the table. They are intelligent animals, and there's plenty of time for high jinks or just plain lounging around. If you were an otter in the Tsitsikamma you could lie on a rock, concealed in the shade, maybe munching a crab, and watch human hikers puffing and panting against the clock with their 50-kilogram (110 pound) packs on the—wait for it—Otter Trail. I'll leave you to work out who's got the best plan.

All you need to be a happy otter is a lake or running river, preferably one that doesn't have *Homo sapiens* dumping chemicals and effluent upstream. You'd want it to be well stocked with crabs, frogs, molluscs and fish, and, as a bonus, you may even be able to live near a river mouth, take the odd dip in the surf, or potter about on the smorgasbord of the intertidal zone. At least for now, the southern and western stretches of coast in South Africa are ideal and relatively pristine, with many river estuaries.

Further north, given the pressure of human populations, things aren't so rosy. That said, the otter is still comfortably on the least endangered list and ranges through most of Africa south of the Sahara, pretty much wherever there is permanent water and bush, with the notable exception of the Congo Basin and the arid areas of Namibia, Botswana and the

Northern Cape. The otters as a whole are represented on every continent except Antarctica.

African clawless otters (a.k.a. Cape clawless otters) are members of the weasel family (Mustelidae) and have the same bright-eyed curiosity as their cousins. They are closely related to badgers and distantly related—though it's probably not something they brag about—to skunks. Unlike their terrestrial cousins, otters are relatively slow and clumsy on land but consummate acrobats in water, propelled along like flexible torpedoes by their powerful tails and partially webbed hind feet. They are more than a match for a mullet. Clawless forepaws are ideal for digging in the sediment and flipping rocks and logs in search of hidden molluscs, worms, crabs and other otter delicacies. They take larger prey to dry land for consumption but do have the endearing and comical habit of occasionally snacking on manageable foods while casually floating on their backs.

Otters are territorial and, by and large, live a solitary life, usually only venturing onto neighboring ranges to find a mate. Home is an underground burrow in an overgrown riverbank, known as a holt, which allows easy access to the aquatic hunting ground and a safe haven if something nasty comes along. Otters have few natural predators, the main ones being pythons and crocodiles, where these creatures occur—another good reason to opt for the southern Cape coast. As usual, among the biggest threats are our rapacious ways. Deforestation in river catchments poses a particularly serious threat to the otter's wellbeing, resulting as it does in erosion and increased turbidity, which, in turn, impacts fish populations, not to mention making it difficult to see prey under water.

December is otter mating season, and once the slap and tickle is over, male (boar) and female (sow) go their separate ways, the female predictably being lumbered with raising the pups. The young are weaned in a couple of months, reach maturity after a year and are then booted out to find their

own way in the world. An otter pup can be almost as long as its mother, and, if they are seen frolicking together, they may be mistaken for a couple.

Adults reach an average of 140 centimeters (55 inches) in overall length, one-third of which is tail, and they tip the scales at anything between 12 and 21 kilograms (26-46 pounds). Their lifespan in the wild is about 10 years, but this can double in the dubious comforts of captivity. They have little or no body fat, despite that relatively large food intake, and rely on their thick, smooth fur, particularly silky on their underbellies, to provide effective insulation in cold water. Although fond of sunbathing, they avoid the midday African heat by spending much of the day in a shady retreat, or in their holt, only venturing out at night and in the cool of morning and evening. In heavily populated or semi-urban areas they tend to be entirely nocturnal, and who can blame them?

WARTHOG

The first warthog was a handsome pig according to African folklore. So much so that he grew narcissistic and arrogant and took perverse pleasure in insulting every animal he came across while trotting about on the African stage. He eventually took things too far by insulting a particularly large lion. To escape the lion's wrath, the warthog plunged head first into an aardvark hole in which a porcupine was having a quiet snooze and promptly got a face full of quills. Unsurprisingly he could find no one willing to help pull them out and was forced to do it himself, so becoming disfigured. Since then he's been pug ugly and only able to land character parts.

Not that this has obstructed a dazzling career. Few people on the planet are unaware of the warthog, at least in his persona as Pumbaa in *The Lion King*, a blockbuster film in which he plays a kind of comical retired sergeant major. His close friend and confidant is played by a wisecracking meerkat. In real life, resting warthogs have been observed allowing banded mongooses to groom them looking for ticks, showing that fact can be just as cute as fiction.

Warthogs are perennials of Africa's savannas and, being diurnal, are invariably seen during a trip to a game reserve, even when all the other prima donnas stay obstinately hidden in the wings. They have a comedy routine that involves running away in single file with their tails stuck up like radio antennas. It may not sound like much, but it usually gets the audience smiling.

Warthogs run away a lot. Apart from lions (presumably still fuming about that ancestral insult), adult warthogs have to run away from a full cast of other villains including leopards, wild dogs, cheetahs and spotted hyenas. Their young also fall prey to Verreaux's eagles, pythons and jackals. When pursued, warthogs head straight for the nearest aardvark burrow, one of several such bolt holes dotted about their home range, all of which have been thoroughly checked out for hidden porcupines. The young dive

straight in, but most adult warthogs slam into reverse at the last minute and enter backwards to put their tusks and their best face forward.

Beauty is in the eye of the beholder, as the saying goes, but maybe it's as well to remember that during life's auditions the beholder is usually having a derogatory snigger behind everyone's back, not just the warthog's. It must be bad enough having a face to sink a thousand ships, without also having to make your way in the world saddled with such an offensive name. Everyone immediately homes in on the facial warts, but they are not really warts at all, not in the warty witch sense; they're bony protuberances. They're there to protect the eyes during battles with other boars to see who gets to play on center stage and land the plum part with the leading lady.

Looks aside, boars can really turn on the charm when it comes to courting, sniffing around everyone's aardvark hole to see who's in the mood. When they get lucky, they approach the object of their desire with a jaunty walk, swinging their hips, tail held high, chomping their jaws, grunting and drooling profusely. If that sounds a tad unromantic, maybe you have to be there, ideally as a female warthog.

A bit over five months later the piglets are born, usually three or four in a litter but sometimes as many as eight. Birth takes place at the onset of the rainy season, which heralds the appearance of new grass, but as usual in nature, there is inevitably a trade-off; the downside is the rain itself, which can come down in buckets and flood the family hole. To avoid this potential catastrophe, the mother immediately shoves the little pigs up onto a kind of pre-prepared mantelpiece, like a row of trophies, just in case. A week later they are up and out in the open, enjoying the grass, and begin little sparring matches to establish who's who in matters pertaining to the order for suckling and trotting behind Mom.

Rather unnecessarily, given that the grass is often bigger than they are, very young warthogs get down on their front knees to feed, just like their parents. Anatomically speaking they are actually bending their wrists, but we don't have to be pedantic about it. You could be forgiven for thinking that they're taking a bow, maybe acknowledging the silent applause that accompanies a performance in survival that has lasted millions of years.

ELAND

During the long, slow plod of evolution every species has to make choices. Some of us turn out sleek and sexy, while others get into an indecisive muddle and, like the platypus and the aardvark, end up looking rather ridiculous. The antelope are no exception. There are curvaceous sports models, such as the springbok and impala, or the dashing sable with it scimitar horns, and then there's the eland. What on earth was it thinking when it put that little head on top of such a humongous body?

Then again, looks aren't everything, and the eland does somehow still manage to exude an air of ponderous gravitas, complete with dewlap, a bit like a Brahman bull.

Finding itself surrounded by carnivores with the latest and greatest in predatory equipment, the eland seems to have surreptitiously torn a leaf from the *Diplodocus* handbook and opted for bulk. It's a pity about the head, but, as the dinosaurs discovered, when trying to keep up with current trends you can't always get everything just right.

The upside of being hefty is that most carnivores, even the big ones, take one look and decide it's probably not worth the effort. Bulking up might mean that you end up being the slowest antelope around, 40 kilometers (25 miles) per hour flat out compared with the springbok's 88 kilometers (55 miles) per hour, but some carnivores are keen on fast food anyway. Cheetahs can get to the head of the queue by belting along at well over 100 kilometers (62 miles) per hour, and wild dogs are prepared to trot behind remorselessly until even the fleetest buck finally runs out of gas. With its cruise control set at about 22 kilometers (14 miles) per hour, the eland can go on forever.

The downside of having a big body is having to eat and eat, then eat some more. Eland are among the least choosy of the antelope when it comes to what they tuck away, being both browsers and grazers: grass, leaves, twigs, fruits, seeds and pods, tubers—bring it on with second helpings. Location is also not that big an issue, and they are equally at home in grasslands, acacia savanna, semi-desert habitat and mountain slopes up to a height of about 4,500 meters (14,800 feet). Their bones have even been found more than halfway up Kilimanjaro, but maybe that was a case of taking a lunch too far. What they don't like are swamps, forest and true desert.

When it was getting equipped the one big problem the eland could never foresee was men with rifles. If you're as big as a barn door and not very fast, you make an easy target. Now that the cordite smoke has cleared the result is balefully obvious, particularly in South Africa. Add the fact that eland are especially susceptible to rinderpest, and it's a relief to find any left at all. Having survived the great slaughter, the few that do remain in the wild are understandably skittish and seldom seen. They purportedly have the longest flight distance of any South African mammal, moving off if a person or a vehicle approaches closer than about 400–500 meters (1300-1600 feet).

The San revered the mighty eland not just as a walking mountain of prime steaks, but as a mystic fellow traveler. The creator god Kaggen's first child was an eland, and he was understandably very fond of it. He chose to manifest himself as one of the great antelope when the mood took him, or perhaps when his praying mantis disguise got a little tight around the middle.

The eland was the central figure in several San rites of passage, including the often difficult and perplexing transition to manhood. Successfully hunting a beast that weighs 20 times as much as you do, using only a dinky bow and arrow, is the stuff of tribal legend. Providing enough meat to feed the family and all the friends and relations for a long, long time was guaranteed to make you popular, not to mention man of the month.

Representations of eland feature prominently in San rock art, painted with a soul-stretching intimacy and sensitivity that clearly shows the pivotal part they must have played in the spiritual and corporeal lives of the artists. The diminutive men and their brushes and paints are long gone, but the art endures, often in secret rocky places where the eland itself still walks, but as a ghost.

CROW

The Norse god Odin had a crow perched on each shoulder, one called Thought and the other Desire. He would send them out each morning to ask questions of the living and the dead, and in this way always knew what was going on. What was routinely going on, at least in the Viking world, was pillaging and bloodshed.

Throughout history, crows could be relied upon to turn up for a public execution and were always the first to arrive to help clean up the carnage on battlefields, the eyes of the slain being a favored delicacy. A gathering of crows was called a "murder," and they inevitably came to be closely associated with death, a reputation helped along by the fact that they were always dressed for the occasion in funereal black.

Crows worked out long ago that human beings are good at killing, not only each other, but just about everything else that flies, crawls or walks. They also observed that we're not always so great at cleaning up the mess afterwards. Keeping up with modern trends, local crows spend a good deal of time patrolling the highways and byways of South Africa, feasting on the birds, mammals and reptiles that have prematurely met their maker under speeding trucks and cars. So bounteous and predictable is this macabre meals-under-wheels service that many now nest on top of convenient roadside telegraph poles. Thanks to their quick wits, they are rarely numbered among the casualties themselves.

South Africa's home-grown family of crows has three members: the pied, the black crow and the white-necked raven, the last-mentioned being by far the largest. Their range extends over almost the entire country, though the raven usually prefers to remain fairly aloof in mountainous terrain, periodically adding to its dodgy reputation as a thug by raiding chicken runs or attacking lambs and disabled sheep. The others make a living wherever opportunities present themselves, from the countryside to suburbia. They will eat just about anything. A piece of rare filet is preferred, but if there's only an overripe banana available, that will do.

All crows are credited with considerable intelligence and excellent memories. Aesop told a fable of a thirsty crow dropping pebbles into a jug of water until the level rose high enough to enable it to drink, thus demonstrating a profound knowledge of the laws of displacement. If you think Aesop was just into tall tales, consider the sobering fact that a similar modern experiment with real crows produced exactly the same result.

Wild crows also seem to have the unnerving ability to recognize individual human faces, notably those of people they can't stand. A conservation official in Durban charged with exterminating a municipal plague of the immigrant house crow, *Corvus splendens*, soon found himself living in a kind of endless sequel to Alfred Hitchcock's film *The Birds*. Given the crows' wily ways, all his attempts at reducing their numbers met with dismal failure, but even out of uniform, walking in a crowd on the street or innocently paddling a canoe on the river, the crows recognized him and let him know of their undying enmity. What was particularly unsettling was that all the crows in the city reacted in the same way, wherever he was, despite the fact that his extermination attempts had been restricted to a few specific locations.

Rather like the Mafia, crows are big on family. Most are social by nature, and interaction with their own kind seems very important to them, particularly for the young and unattached. They usually pair for life, and when breeding time rolls round, juveniles from the previous year sometimes help their parents gather nesting material. Thereafter, both parents take turns incubating the eggs and caring for the chicks.

Like the Mafia, they also purportedly hold their own courts, presumably to try transgressors of the crow code. Weird assemblies of crows have been observed at various times and places forming a circle around one of their luckless peers. The croaking and crowing continues for some considerable time, and then suddenly, as if on a given signal, all the members of the assembly pounce on the individual in the center and peck him to death. They then disperse and fly away.

"Once upon a midnight dreary" begins Edgar Allen Poe's poem *The Raven*, and it doesn't get much more cheerful than that.

DUGONG

The sailors of old, or perhaps short-sighted old sailors, regularly confused dugongs and manatees with mermaids. It's understandable. In the days of sailing ships the crew were often at sea for months on end, and during all that time there was never a fair maid in sight. Even the wizened first mate picking at the remains of his rotten teeth with the tip of a rusty marlin spike probably started to look attractive. So when the ship dropped anchor and a dugong rose from the sea, coquettishly shaking its whiskers, there must indeed have been a stampede to the ship's rail amid a cacophony of wolf whistles.

On his first voyage to America, Christopher Columbus wrote in his journal that he had quite distinctly seen three mermaids. He was off the coast of Haiti at the time, and to be fair he did also note, with more than a hint of disappointment, that he didn't think they were particularly beautiful, having rather masculine features.

Salty yarns aside, a much more likely outcome of such encounters is that the sailors would have done their level best to capture the dugong and haul it aboard, not to wine and dine it and shower it with roses but to slaughter the inoffensive beast for its oil and delicious meat. The dugongs of the East African coast have been hunted virtually to extinction, as has the African manatee, its close relation on the West Coast of Africa. Although they are both now legally protected, gills nets and illegal hunting still take their toll on the remaining small populations. The last dugong bastion is Australia's vast coast, which is home to about 80,000 of these mammals.

Dugongs are air-breathing and live in the warm coastal waters of the Indian Ocean, including the Red Sea and the Persian Gulf, and along the western edges of the Pacific, while their cousins the manatees hug the Atlantic shores of the Americas and West Africa. The name dugong is derived from a Malaysian word meaning "lady of the sea," perhaps intended to encapsulate their demure and gentle nature rather than any real or imagined feminine charms. A more literal translation, however, is "lady in an outdoor bath," which does have a faintly voyeuristic ring to it.

The dugong is thankfully unaware of its role in the fantasies of sex-starved mariners. It lives a placid life, grazing on sea grass meadows in the coastal shallows, and has little in the way of natural enemies. Although capable of bursts of speed up to about 25 knots, the dugong's rotund shape is its principal defense, particularly against sharks; it simply turns its ample back on them, a bit like a society matron freezing out an undesirable at a village fête. The young do occasionally fall prey to sharks or saltwater crocodiles but these days are probably more likely to meet their end in a gill net or a collision with a motorboat.

Dugongs are social mammals and usually live in family groups of 3–10 individuals, although periodic large gatherings of up to 500 do occur where the population allows. The last such gathering off the coast of East Africa was observed in the 1960s, and such a sight is highly unlikely to be seen there again. Fewer than 200 now remain in Mozambique's Bazaruto Archipelago, and no reinforcements are on the way. They are semi-nomadic but, by and large, stay in the same general area their whole lives, moving slowly up and down the coast, drifting in and out with the tides to where they hope the grass is greener still.

Their long-term survival prospects are not enhanced by the fact that they are excruciatingly slow breeders, to some extent regulating reproduction according to the availability of sea grass, which is itself vulnerable to coastal pollution and trawling. A female dugong only gives

birth to a single chubby baby every 5–7 years, after a 14-month gestation. At least eight years and more will pass before the newborn eventually reaches sexual maturity, longer than is typical of most other mammals. On the upside, if they can avoid catastrophic motorboat encounters and other artificial perils, dugongs can look forward to a long and hopefully uneventful life, a lucky few grazing through into their late sixties.

Despite the fact that even at a distance they are unlikely to be confused with Marilyn Monroe, dugongs seem to have captured the romantic imagination of more than just frustrated western mariners. In India their meat is believed to be an aphrodisiac, while in parts of Thailand people are convinced that dugong tears make a powerful love potion. Given the perilous future we've made for them, if dugongs ever cry, they most likely shed bitter tears of anguish.

BOOMSLANG

Ever since the apple tree incident in the Garden of Eden, snakes have been taking the rap for humanity's misfortunes. The boomslang is no exception, being particularly arboreal and seductively handsome.

If that's not enough, the snake is supposed to make a habit of dropping from trees onto rural pedestrians with the express purpose of biting them, a task it fails to perform with unerring consistency. It may, of course, be that boomslangs don't want to put themselves in harm's way by attacking a large inedible biped, a point that we tend to overlook in our stick-waving moods of righteous indignation. That said, in Africa there are lots of trees and lots of pedestrians and from time to time accidents do happen. Even in these rare instances, the snake is far more likely to mumble an apology and slither on its way than to bite.

The number of recorded fatalities notched up against the boomslang in the past 50 years would barely reach double figures, and most of the victims were professional snake handlers.

While Africans have always known that the boomslang is highly venomous, western herpetologists largely pooh-poohed this opinion until one of their number, Karl Schmidt, was bitten in 1957 by a juvenile he was casually and confidently handling. To his enduring credit Mr. Schmidt carefully recorded what subsequently happened to him, a consummate professional to the very, fatal end. He had clearly never read Agatha Christie's 1935 novel, *Death in the Clouds*. It was the butler that did it, in the library, with a boomslang.

The boomslang is a member of the poisonous but otherwise happy family of Columbridae, but it is the only member that has the teeth and the chemical cocktail capable of delivering a bite fatal to humans. Its venom is primarily a slow-acting hemotoxin that switches off the body's blood-clotting system and causes internal hemorrhaging, including in the brain. Symptoms are slow to appear, so that someone who has been bitten may start to relax, think it's no big deal and not pop along to the doctor.

151

This is a serious mistake. Without antivenom, the only cure is a total blood transfusion and, if left for two or three days, even that may come too late.

Another misconception, arising from the snake's petite features, has led some to believe that it is physically incapable of opening its mouth wide enough to bite anything bigger than a toe or finger. In fact, it can open its jaws up to 170 degrees, which is more than enough to bring the back fangs into action on an arm or a leg.

But enough of the scary stuff; the boomslang is a shy and retiring snake, certainly worthy of caution and respect but not to be feared. It is notoriously difficult to see, let alone catch, preferring to glide away through the branches rather than confront its tormentor. While boomslangs may come to the ground in pursuit of prey, they are arboreal snakes and will always return to a tree to enjoy their meal.

Newborn boomslangs are totally harmless to humans. They appear to have wriggled straight out of a Disney cartoon—gray with blue speckles and gigantic eyes that take up virtually the whole of their tiny heads. They start at about 20 centimeters (8 inches) in length out of the egg and seldom grow to an adult length of more than 170 centimeters (67 inches). Adult coloration varies considerably, and they are among the few snakes in which the color of male and female differs. Females are usually brown, while, confusingly, males can be green, black, gray or yellow; even the occasional pink one has been observed.

The adult snake's large eyes remain its most distinctive identifying feature. Unlike other species, boomslangs are thought to have binocular vision and are able to see their prey even when it is stationary. The slow and super-cautious progress of the chameleon, a favorite prey species, is consequently not much of a defense.

Unlike us, weaver birds have genuine cause to bear a grudge against the boomslang. It is very partial to their eggs, their chicks and, given the opportunity, the birds themselves. To add insult to injury, in the cold snaps of winter boomslangs are also inclined to commandeer a cozy nest in which to hibernate—a very literal case of being eaten out of house and home.

GUINEAFOWL

The Lugbara people, who live in Uganda, make good use of guineafowls in their cooking pots and also in their many proverbs. Excessive pride made the guineafowl's head go bald, they say, meaning that presumption inevitably leads to humiliation. Oddly enough, another Lugbara proverb ascribes the bird's baldness to its being overly shy, proving that for every good proverb there is often another one to cancel it out.

In England's green and pleasant land the chatter of guineafowl presages sunshine and good luck, while in the pragmatic USA, free-range chicken farmers like to have them around, because they are better at spotting incoming eagles than the easily distracted domestic hen. Wherever they are, guineafowl make excellent sentries, setting up a cackling racket whenever they spot any kind of trespasser, airborne or otherwise, and even when they don't. Given the bird's propensity to let rip for their own social reasons, one has to make allowance for a lot of false alarms.

The birds were first domesticated in the lands around the Gulf of Guinea, and so choosing a name was a no-brainer. That said, under various local names they have been providing a reliable source of wild meat and eggs throughout Africa since time immemorial. They feature prominently in African art and are proudly, if rather repetitively, displayed on modern souvenirs from Africa, especially such mundane items as dishcloths, tea trays, place mats, oven gloves, salt and pepper pots, serving spoons, aprons, serviettes, tee shirts...you get the picture.

South Africa is home to two species: the helmeted or crowned guineafowl and the crested. The former is traditionally an inhabitant of thorny scrub and savanna but is now seen all over the place, equally at ease in farmlands and in the leafy suburbs of cities throughout the country, wherever there is a reliable water supply. By contrast, the crested guineafowl is coyly confined in South Africa to the northern half of KwaZulu-Natal and northern Limpopo, where it spends most of its time in riverine bush and secondary forest and is far more shy and retiring than its peripatetic cousin.

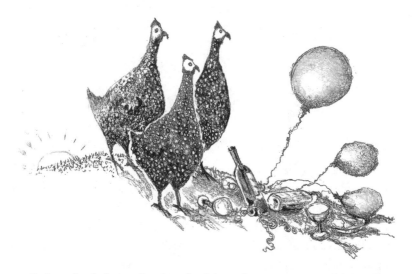

Quite why helmeted guineafowl have been so successful in adapting to suburban living is something of a mystery. They have an unnerving propensity for running away from a speeding motor car only to abruptly change their minds and run straight back in front of it. Given the current standard of driving, that alone should have put them on the road to extinction. But the probable explanation lies in the total absence of jackals, pythons, large raptors and all the other predators that enjoy a plump guineafowl every bit as much as the Lugbaras.

The main visual difference between the two species is suggested by their names. The crested has a thick bunch of curly feathers on the top of its head, while the helmeted sports a bony crown that varies slightly in shape in different regions of South Africa. There are no obvious differences between the sexes of either species, and, by and large, they peck their way through the same menu. This consists of a wide variety of insects, snails, seeds, bulbs, worms and ticks. The helmeted sticks to the ground when feeding, while the crested is known to occasionally flap up into trees to feed on fruit.

Both species form large, noisy flocks, sometimes numbering in the hundreds. They break up into smaller groups when the birds go to roost in trees at night, reassembling the next morning. During the breeding season (from October to February) they stick to small family groups until the chicks have grown.

They are essentially terrestrial birds and usually fly only to reach a roost or, as a last resort, to escape a predator if running very fast fails.

Neither species is a great nest builder, a simple scrape in the ground under a secluded bush or hedge sufficing. A clutch of 6–8 eggs is usually laid and incubated for 23 days. The young birds can fly after only 14 days, which may be just as well for the suburban dwellers. Hatching time is a bonanza for domestic cats, particularly those who have grown mighty tired of a monotonous diet of canned sardines.

The Ancient Greeks used to obtain the birds from North Africa, and the scientific name for the helmeted guineafowl is *Numida melegaris*, deriving from Meleagar, a mythical Greek hero. According to legend, Meleagar killed his uncles in an argument and was, in turn, slain by his own mother. His sisters were so upset by these alarming goings-on—and no doubt making quite a racket about it—that the goddess Artemis decided to turn them all into guineafowl. The distinctive white spots on the birds' dark plumage represent their tears.

BARN OWL

Nailing a dead owl to the barn door was one popular and predictably useless method of warding off evil on the farm in medieval Europe. In our own more enlightened times the barn owl is encouraged to set up home in the barn, even to the extent of the farmer cutting a hole in the eaves to give easy access to the rafters.

The reason for this agrarian about-turn lies in the realization that barn owls consume vast quantities of rodents, particularly mice, which might otherwise get stuck into the seed stocks and adversely affect the farmer's bottom line. The owls' close nocturnal association with witches and warlocks is now politely overlooked, or more likely dismissed as the nonsense it always was.

In many African cultures, owls in general, and the common barn owl in particular, are viewed as harbingers of bad luck, ill health and death and are associated with the seamier side of the black arts. The Balozi people, who live in the Caprivi Strip, believe that owls induce disease merely by being in the neighborhood, while the Shona of Zimbabwe traditionally regard them as witches' birds. In Afrikaans the barn owl is sometimes known as a *doodsvoël*, which translates as "death bird." This gloomy label arises from the belief that when the owl emits its eerie call from the roof of a house in which one of the inhabitants is already dying, death is sure to follow.

The great big eyes and the thousand-yard stare contribute to the sense of unease that many folk feel in the presence of owls. Add a teacher's mortarboard to its head, which illustrators of children's books often seem compelled to do, and you really feel as though you've been summoned to the headmaster's office.

An owl never looks at you from the corner of its eye; it always swivels its head to confront you head-on, if it deigns to look at you at all. The reason isn't outrage or indignation but simply that it has to do that. Owls don't have swivelling eyeballs; instead they have eye barrels, elongated tubes held in place by bony structures in the skull called "sclerotic rings." To make up for it, they can swivel their head a full and disconcerting 270 degrees. They have binocular vision and are able to see objects in three dimensions and judge distances as we do, but let's be honest, it's a bit like comparing our cheap knock-offs with their top-of-the-range Celestron SkyMasters.

Despite their impressive optical equipment, barn owls, like their strictly nocturnal cousins, rely on their hearing more than their eyesight to locate prey. The ear openings on either side of the head are asymmetrical so that a sound from above or below reaches one ear a tiny fraction of a second after the other. They are able to do the complicated math instantly and, by moving their head from side to side and up and down, can pinpoint the target, betrayed by a squeak or a rustle in the leaves, with astonishing accuracy.

Barn owls are in the Tytonidae, a separate family from the other owls, on the basis of anatomical differences and their distinct facial characteristics. They look as though they're peering out of a nun's habit (hence their other Afrikaans name, *nonnetjie-uil* or "nun bird,") rather than through the pair of professorial spectacles preferred by many other owls.

Two species of the family occur in southern Africa: the ubiquitous barn owl and the grass owl, which is limited to Africa south of the equator. Barn owls occur just about everywhere in Africa, except for the Sahara and the dense forests of the Democratic Republic of the Congo, and also occur throughout the rest of the world, with the exception of the extreme latitudes.

The grass owl has a very different lifestyle from its slightly smaller and more abundant close relative. It lives and nests in long grass in lightly wooded country, especially near streams and vleis[3]. By contrast, the barn owl often makes use of various artificial structures where it can gain easy access to dark, sheltered corners, such as mine tunnels, church towers and the lofts of buildings. Deserted hamerkop nests and caves are also favored nesting and roosting sites.

One other peculiarity is that the barn owl usually lays its eggs at relatively long intervals, so that in a given brood the eldest bird may already have its feathers and be agitating for the car keys by the time the last egg is laid. Other owls follow more normal egg-laying procedures, though it has been noted that the chicks in a grass owl's brood can also

---

3 A vlei (Afrikaans) is low marshy ground that feeds a stream or a small marsh or shallow minor lake that could be seasonal.

vary considerably in size.

The barn owl has a vocabulary that consists mainly of screams, snores and other creepy sounds. This repertoire, together with its nocturnal lifestyle, and the fact that it often spends the day in dark recesses where vampires and bogeymen routinely hang out, is the main reason that the bird features so prominently in Halloween superstitions and folklore.

According to old English tradition, concoctions made from owls' eggs are supposed to cure alcoholism, whooping cough and, predictably, improve eyesight. Strangely, or perhaps fortunately for the owl, no such remedies could claim to instill wisdom.

CROCODILE

"How doth the little crocodile..." begins a short poem in Lewis Carroll's *Alice in Wonderland*. The answer is that it doth fairly well, all things considered. It has been welcoming little fishes into its gently smiling jaws for well over 60 million years and still manages to cling tenaciously to the IUCNs Least Concern list.

Crocodiles are routinely portrayed in folklore and literature as cold-hearted, duplicitous scoundrels, including in Carroll's sardonic little verse. Budding naturalists in the Middle Ages were partly responsible for setting the tone in their bestiaries and encyclopedias, punting the idea that crocodiles hypocritically weep in a blood-curdling display of phony remorse while devouring their victims. Shakespeare and other Elizabethan dramatists regularly seized on this imagery when making a point about their own unsavory villains. Nowadays the phrase "shedding crocodile tears" is usually and understandably reserved for newspaper articles about politicians.

As far as the crocodile is concerned, it is simply eating lunch. If it could give a damn, it would probably be perplexed at the sanctimonious opprobrium heaped upon its broad and scaly back and might well ponder where the real hypocrisy lies. It does indeed cry, mainly to lubricate its eyes, and there is some evidence that the act of eating can occasionally induce an incidental flow of tears. But anyone who has tucked into a particularly hot and spicy crocodile curry will be familiar with that phenomenon—it has to do with heat and sinuses rather than emotion.

The crocodile's image as a stealthy mugger is not helped along by the fact that it is stealthy and it is a mugger, lying in deadly and watery wait for unsuspecting passers-by. Mugger is another name for the marsh crocodile, claimed by some to be a corruption of the Hindi word *magar*, which means "water monster." This species lives in the Indian subcontinent and is closely related to the Nile crocodile. Muggers are infamous for balancing bundles of twigs on their snouts during the nest-building season in an attempt to

lure waterbirds to within snapping range. They are not, by and large, held up as shining examples of moral rectitude, least of all in Rudyard Kipling's *Jungle Book* stories.

Though their numbers continue to dwindle, Nile crocodiles are still widely distributed in tropical African rivers and lakes. A few grow to awesome proportions, particularly in East Africa, reaching 5 or 6 meters (16-20 feet) from stem to stern and weighing more than a ton. South Africa is home to a few celebrity behemoths, but the majority of mature adult crocodiles in the wilds of southern Africa are less than 3 meters (10 feet) in length—still big enough to make a meal of large and unwary mammals, including people daft or unlucky enough to take a dip in their watery domain.

Crocodiles eat anything with meat on it, but their diet begins with modest fare. Hatchlings make do with tadpoles, frogs, insects and small fish, graduating to more substantial meals as they grow larger. Fish, especially catfish, form the main staple for most young crocodiles— no big surprises there, given that they share the same habitat. In their very early years they fall prey to a variety of other predators themselves, including fish eagles, snakes and adult crocodiles, which are not above snacking on their little nephews and nieces. Crocodiles only reach maturity at 12 and in ideal circumstances can live to be 100. Many years will therefore pass before a hatchling can hope to join the big bruisers assembled for events like the annual wildebeest migration across the Mara River in Tanzania.

Despite their heartless reputation, crocodiles are attentive mothers, at least in the limited sense of watching over their eggs and giving a helping hand with hatching. They need to be attentive, as many eggs are stolen by monitor lizards, baboons and other opportunists, with estimates putting this as high as 90 percent in some areas. And while they are generally thought to be loners, crocodiles are in fact quite social in a snappy, mind-my-space sort of way, even cooperating once in a while to herd fish: they use the sweep of their tails in a slow-motion variant of the brainy dolphin's flamboyant and more complicated method.

In recent years, crocodiles and their American cousins, the alligators, have ventured into the luxury goods business. The downside of this radical departure is that they are the luxury goods. Their skins are widely used to make high-end handbags, shoes and other fashion accessories, while their meat finds its way onto a few select restaurant menus to satisfy the needs of curious, dry-eyed diners.

Crocodile farms are now big business. The only upside for the crocodile in having *Homo sapiens* as a midwife is that close to 80 percent of the eggs hatch, and, barring diseases, most of the hatchlings survive. This has been particularly good news for alligators, thousands of which are released back into the wild each year in the Americas, where they had previously been hunted virtually to extinction. It is not a dignified state of affairs, but then again crocodilians are accustomed to surviving global ecological catastrophes, including the meteor that totaled the dinosaurs, and we are but the latest one.

MOLE-RAT

The annual convention of African mole-rats is an event that fortunately never happens. If it did, there would probably be a lot of infighting and turf disputes. Even worse, the proceedings would continually be disrupted by the startling appearance of a naked East African streaker.

Though the various species of African mole-rat share similar lifestyles, they are as different from each other as politicians and honest men. To add to the confusion, nobody seems to be completely sure just how many distinct species there actually are.

The naked mole-rat—and never did a name more succinctly describe its owner—lives in the sandy soils of East Africa, in communities modeled more on those of ants and termites than other mammals. A single breeding female and one or two sexually active males hold sway over a huge colony that can number up to 300. If you're not the queen or one of her studs, you're a worker, harvesting roots and tubers for the communal larder, or a soldier, charged with seeing off any unwanted visitors. The queen mole-rat keeps everyone's mind off sex and focused on the tasks at hand by her social behavior, rather than by emitting a pheromone as some insects do.

In stark contrast, Cape dune mole-rats keep their clothes on, are a whole lot bigger and live solitary and cantankerous lifestyles. They have been causing havoc with transport and agriculture in the soft coastal sands of South Africa's Western Cape since the days of Jan van Riebeeck, who moaned about them in his journal in the 1600s. Using their clawed forefeet, they are mighty earthmovers and miners. A single individual can push up 500 kilograms (1100 pounds) of soil each month into many large sand mounds, excavating and maintaining an exclusive burrow system extending for 200–300 meters (650-1000 feet).

They are also fiercely territorial and drum on the wall of their private tunnel if they sense a neighbour getting too close, not unlike the solitary grump in the next-door apartment who wants you to turn the music down. During the breeding season the drumming changes pitch and volume, taking on an altogether more desperate tone that is even audible above ground. Connubial interludes are short and to the point, and the 2–3 pups that are born can't wait to get away from Mom and each other after a mere couple of months.

Demurely placed between these super-social and antisocial opposites, common mole-rats try to lead a more-or-less normal family life, as much as that's possible when you need to spend so much of your time digging tunnels with your teeth. They live in colonies numbering up to 14 individuals, comprising a breeding pair and their offspring, though non-breeding house guests sometimes get to join the group. More widespread than any other African mole-rat, their subterranean kingdom extends across most of South Africa, Zimbabwe and the southern half of Mozambique.

Unlike moles, all mole-rats are vegetarian, feeding mainly on roots and tubers and, in a few cases, dragging down the whole plant, partly to eat and partly to use for nesting material. They can all happily munch their way through plants that are toxic to man and beast. Finding food is easier for some than for others, depending on where they live, a factor that helps to determine the social systems and domestic arrangements developed by different species.

Mole-rats spend almost their entire lives underground and are surprisingly well organized, excavating sleeping quarters, larders and toilet areas, apart from their vast array of foraging tunnels. They can beetle backwards almost as fast as they can forwards, which is pretty essential when the tunnel diameter isn't much wider than you are.

Despite this orderly approach and attention to personal hygiene, the atmosphere below ground gets pretty toxic, even worse than a locker room after a rugby match, particularly for the large mobs of naked mole-rats. If you were miniaturized and popped down to visit them you would pass out in about 60 seconds and pass away a minute or two later.

The ability of mole-rats not simply to survive but to flourish in a low oxygen/high carbon dioxide environment has intrigued scientists, and particularly so in the case of naked mole-rats, because they live for a remarkably long time, up to 20 times as long as fresh-air rodents of comparable size. Some individuals of this species have been taking part in longevity studies in labs around the world for over 30 years and are still going strong. They don't get tumors, cancers or age in the same way as we do, staying fighting fit and feisty virtually all their lives. If it's any consolation, they are saggy-skinned and quite repulsive to start with, so much so that, ironically, Eduard Rüppell, the 19th-century naturalist who first described them, thought they were mutated or diseased examples of another species.

Foul air aside, life underground is safe and secure by and large, though mole-rats have to conduct regular repairs and maintenance to deal with rain and surface-impact damage. A predator may detect them from the surface and start digging, but mole-rats can run away through their tunnels and, as a last resort, have a pre-prepared escape tunnel to take them much deeper underground. No self-respecting jackal or hyena wants to spend the whole afternoon shoveling dirt to get down that far, as tasty a morsel as a mole-rat might be.

The main underground predator problem is snakes. Cobras and mole snakes, to name but two, take their fair share, but the real danger comes when mole-rats have to leave their tunnels and travel across the surface. This happens mainly when the young disperse, usually after the onset of rains, to find their own subterranean patch. If they're unlucky, a small army of potential predators stands ready to snap them up, including raptors and just about every other carnivore that happens to be in the right place at the right time. In suburban areas, swimming pools are a deep and present danger.

Although these little troglodytes don't generally impress with their looks, they play an important role in helping to aerate and drain the soil and in preventing the overpopulation of plant and animal species. If you believe the enthusiastic papers delivered at medical conventions from time to time, they may yet help solve some of our most pressing problems in cancer research and gerontology.

WHITE PELICAN

Pelicans were regarded as models of parental devotion and self-sacrifice by medieval religious thinkers. A popular motif in religious texts, carved in wood and stone or incorporated into the stained-glass windows of churches and cathedrals, showed the laudable bird pecking her own breast to supply her young with blood. A grislier version of the story, borrowed in part from Egyptian mythology, tells us that pelican chicks attack their mother, who totally loses it and retaliates by killing them. Filled with remorse and compassion, the parent bird then brings her delinquent brood back to life by wounding herself and showering them with her own blood. In this way the pelican became a powerful symbol of redemption from sin.

Quite where this daft and gory fantasy came from is anyone's guess. Perhaps some ancient birder, in the days long before binoculars were available, spotted a pelican on her nest dribbling fish guts and misinterpreted what he was seeing. Be that as it may, the behavior of real pelicans bears little resemblance to that of their idealized ecclesiastical alter egos, which is not to say that they are bad parents, or at least no better or worse than most of their avian peers. In southern Africa, their main problem is finding a suitable nesting site at which to be any kind of parent.

White pelicans are big birds with exacting needs. An adult male can weigh as much as 15 kilograms (33 pounds) and have a wingspan in excess of 3 meters (10 feet), plus of course there's that whopping, one-of-a-kind beak. It takes a lot of protein to keep such a hefty assembly airworthy, and fish are harder and harder to find these days.

That's not their only problem. White pelicans nest in colonies on the ground in southern Africa and don't like to be disturbed. They are far from inconspicuous and hence need nesting sites out of reach of potential predators, typically jackals and hyenas. An uninhabited island in a freshwater lake is ideal, but those aren't easy to find either. One such fine estate in Namibia proved to be ephemeral, as the birds discovered to their cost. As summer rolled on, the waters gradually evaporated and eager

predators watching from the shore were eventually able to wade over to the nesting site without even having to roll up their trousers.

Fortunately, pelicans are superb fliers, effortlessly covering more than 100 kilometers (62 miles) each day to and from freshwater fishing grounds, so an offshore island, like Dassen Island off the southwest coast of South Africa, presents a viable option. Here, the pelican colony shares the space with family-minded gannets, Cape cormorants and kelp gulls, among others. We all know that neighbors can be a problem, especially when they're raising noisy kids, but the pelicans have adopted a dark way of dealing with that: they eat the chicks, and even, on occasion, the other birds themselves.

Pelicans normally eat fish and prefer larger ones weighing half a kilogram (1 pound) and more. They often use a cooperative hunting method, seven or eight birds working in tandem and forming a semicircle in fairly shallow water to trap a shoal of fish. That famous elastic pouch is then put to work as a highly effective scoop. In ideal conditions, where fish are abundant, they can eat their fill within a relatively short time and spend the rest of the day preening and relaxing.

Times are tough in southern Africa, and the Dassen Island colony's behavior is unusual by international standards, but far from unique. In 2006 a white pelican in London's Hyde Park casually grabbed and swallowed a live pigeon to the utter disbelief and consternation of a gaggle of genteel afternoon strollers. Elsewhere, from Australia to Mexico, pelicans of various species have been observed catching and eating seabirds and other unusual prey from time to time. In southern Africa, the alternative diet seems to have become routine rather than opportunistic, not just on Dassen Island but also off Walvis Bay. The pelicans have even adapted their cooperative fish-hunting method when wading into cormorant and gannet colonies. Like it or not they seem to be doing well on this untraditional diet to the extent that their modest numbers have increased slightly in recent years.

When they're attending to their own intimate family matters, white pelicans usually lay two eggs, but more often than not only one chick makes it to maturity. The other dies, a victim of sibling rivalry and parental neglect. Notwithstanding the philosophical musings of medieval wishful thinkers, if the parent pelicans are upset by this routine natural tragedy, they keep it to themselves.

BABOON

Baboons usually make the news for all the wrong reasons, but once upon a long time ago they worked in law enforcement. Ancient Egyptian art depicts baboons helping cops in pleated skirts hunt down criminals and control unruly crowds. They were also popular as pets, and there is some evidence that they helped with the fig harvest.

In recent times, South African literature has been lightly peppered with examples of Chacma baboons behaving like model citizens. We can read about Jack, a captive male baboon who helped his crippled master with his railway signalman's duties near Uitenhage, even collecting a salary of sorts from the railway company. The self-impressed French explorer Le Vaillant tells quaint tales in his memoirs about his long-suffering baboon companion, many of which unintentionally put the baboon in a much better light than him. In *The Plains of Camdeboo*, author Eve Palmer tells us about conscientious baboon shepherds, while Eugène Marais, the biggest baboon fan by far, regales us with many quasi-metaphysical yarns about their enigmatic natures.

The occurrence of these cozy inter-species interludes has not, by and large, extended into the present day. Baboons living in close proximity to humans have long rap sheets that list an embarrassing array of offenses: breaking and entering, larceny, malicious damage to property, lewd behavior and even kidnapping. To be fair to the baboons, a good many charges are probably trumped up or at least exaggerated, particularly the one about kidnapping. While there have been isolated reports of baboons snatching human babies, notably by the inexhaustible Mr. Marais, they have invariably given them back intact, rarely demanding much in the way of a ransom.

Baboons are not territorial, a difficult concept for human beings to grasp, saddled as many of us are with a whopping mortgage and an inordinate pride in our herbaceous borders. They basically hang out wherever there's a reliable food supply and somewhere safe to sleep at night, seeing no

reason to move until they're pushed out. As our suburban mini-empires extend remorselessly into the wild lands, baboons have tended to become felons by default. Bungalows popping up in their home range, replete with well-stocked kitchens and delicious transplants from the local garden center, must seem heaven-sent. It must be equally perplexing to find these treats fiercely defended by red-faced homeowners with yapping dogs.

Away from human populations, baboons continue to live their lives blissfully unaware of the need to conform to our social norms. Troops typically consist of about 50–60 individuals, though much larger groups are unexceptional. Baboons are big believers in the safety-in-numbers principle, a sensible precaution given that they feature prominently in the diet of a variety of predators. Leopards, lions and spotted hyenas head the list, while jackals, pythons, eagles and other carnivorous opportunists bring up the rear, taking a steady toll on the young. Only 30 percent, on average, make it to maturity.

Baboons lead complex social lives, intricate and varied enough to support or implode any number of complicated or airy-fairy theories. There's no doubt that adult males sort themselves into a dominance hierarchy, those with the biggest bulk and canines and the most testosterone predictably ending up at the top of the heap. Fights resulting in death or permanent, debilitating injuries are the exception; the opposition is more usually chased, stared or grimaced into submission. Troop females also form a hierarchy, though this, as one would expect of the ladies, is much more subtle and tends to fluctuate depending upon each individual's reproductive status.

To boggling human eyes, female baboons are the scandalous Lolitas of the bushveld. A female can come into estrus at any time of the year, the bright red, swollen skin on her rump advertising her sexual readiness every bit as ostentatiously as a back-street prostitute waving a garish plastic handbag. She solicits intercourse by flashing the whites of her eyelids and presenting her rump to virtually any male who looks even faintly interested. Not all are, least of all the dominant male, who waits until he's sure she's ready to conceive. Everyone else then has to back off, so to speak.

In an attempt to squeeze a little romance from this rather sordid reproductive saga, researchers have pointed out that females sometimes consort with a single male for several days during estrus, during which time they sleep and forage close to one another. The male in question may or may not end up as the father of her baby, but he does stand by her as a long-term friend and ally.

Despite the zillions of binoculars trained on the bush at any given moment, the birth of a baby baboon has rarely been witnessed. The female likes her privacy, and birthing usually takes place in a secluded spot at night.

There are very few critters cuter than an infant baboon. In a recent incident captured on camera, even a lioness who had just bloodily massacred a baby's mother turned sentimental, so it's little wonder that the whole troop takes an interest in bringing up junior, including, notably, dominant males, who seem particularly fond of playing with babies. But like everything else in the baboon world, things are usually not that simple. There are jealousies and squabbles, and it pays a mother to have built up strong social bonds with one or more male baboons. If a tetchy, high-ranking female takes an abusive interest in her baby, the mother can hopefully rely on his intervention.

A large troop of baboons has little to fear during the day as it forages in the savanna. Even lions will usually back off when confronted by a defensive group of large males. The night is another story, and baboons make sure they are safely bedded down in a large tree or on a precipitous rocky cliff well before sunset. If you creep up on them from below, they will likely give one final demonstration of their contempt for human social niceties by urinating on your head.

PORCUPINE

If you happened to be in a local restaurant and overheard the people at the next table talking about the Porcupettes, you might assume that your fellow diners were discussing a chubby female pop group. Instead they would in all likelihood be referring to the offspring of *Hystrix africaeaustralis*, the Cape porcupine, a rodent whose musical repertoire is confined to unmelodious snuffles, growls and quill-rattling. Despite this limitation, porcupines sometimes feature in the frequently opaque lyrics of popular music and have even bestowed their name on a progressive rock group that has incidentally enjoyed international fame and fortune in recent years.

Like most pop stars, porcupines are mainly nocturnal and enjoy considerable, though far less visible, success around the world. Vietnam is the only place where they're locally endangered, as people there eat too many of them.

Cape porcupines are members of the Old World porcupine family and live throughout Africa, with close relatives in southern Europe and Asia. More distantly related is the New World family, members of which live in North America and the northern areas of South America. The New World porcupines are differentiated by having their quills embedded separately, among other things, as opposed to the clusters sported by the Cape porcupine. American porcupines are also fond of climbing trees to feed on fruit, which seems a remarkably daring thing to do if you're covered in sharp spikes.

The name porcupine derives from the old French *porc espin*, which means "pig with spines." Being rodents, they are not remotely related to pigs, but their quills are without doubt their most prominent feature. The quills are sharp, can be up to 30 centimeters (12 inches) long and are more than a major nuisance if you're a predator trying to eat one of these creatures. Despite this, porcupines are preyed upon by a surprising number of other animals, including leopards, lions, rock pythons and even honey badgers. Some predators are more adept than others at coping with

the prickly problems that inevitably arise, and all of them run the risk of being seriously incapacitated and ultimately killed by their meal.

Rock pythons seem particularly unlikely adversaries, but if they get the angles right they can happily squeeze the life out of a porcupine and then eat it headfirst, the backward-facing quills conveniently flattening in the right direction as the meal goes down. Being skewered by a few quills during the constricting process is normally not a fatal issue. The main problem comes if the python is disturbed once it has gone through all the effort of swallowing the porcupine and then tries to regurgitate its meal, as it instinctively does in an emergency. That inevitably ends in disaster. The snake also needs to choose a spot for its traditional after-dinner nap rather carefully—falling even a short distance off the rocks can be disastrous, what with a distended belly full of keratin needles.

The big cats usually fare reasonably well, so much so that porcupines form a small but significant percentage of the diet of lions and leopards in some areas. Care, as always, is the watchword. Quills deeply embedded in the mouth or paws can make eating and walking difficult or even impossible, all the more so if the wounds turn septic. More often than not, though, the cats get it right, and a face full of quills is not always the disaster it may appear to be. Unlike their New World cousins, the quills of Cape porcupines are not barbed and can fall out or be dislodged with due care and diligence.

Porcupines defend themselves as best they can, but on the whole are shy and unaggressive creatures. They are sometimes solitary, but the normal family unit consists of a monogamous pair and their offspring. During the day they hide away in aardvark burrows, where such are available, and where not, in caves and rock crevices.

They're vegetarians, eating a wide variety of plant material including bulbs, fruit, seeds, roots and bark. They can be a pest as crop raiders in some areas, notably in Kenya where subsistence farmers have responded by adding them as a delicacy to the village menu. They also gnaw bones, crave salt and are occasionally attracted to campsite toilets by the smell of urea, probably something to bear in mind during your next hurried nocturnal visit to a long drop in the bush.

Porcupines don't feature prominently on the usual lunatic lists of animal-part aphrodisiacs, unlike the poor rhino with its low libido. This is fortunate but strange, as the one big thing a porcupine can look forward to in life is regular sex. The happy pair indulges in sexual behavior every day, initiated by the female as a form of social bonding and to maintain her cycle. Subordinate females may get in on the action now and again but do not conceive.

Despite this daily activity, the breeding couple usually produces only one litter each year, comprising between one and three offspring. More often than not the result is a single, no doubt charming but decidedly uncuddly, porcupette.

EGYPTIAN GOOSE

The Great Honker was another name for the Egyptian creator god Gengen Wer who took the form of a goose and—apparently without undue stress or strain—laid the golden egg from which the sun hatched. With such impressive credentials, the Egyptian goose was inevitably regarded as sacred in Ancient Egypt, though sanctity didn't exclude these birds from having to contribute to a roast lunch. They were kept as domestic poultry by the Egyptians, as they were by both the Romans and Greeks, and featured prominently in their art.

In our own times of remorseless lists and reclassifications we are told that the Egyptian goose is not a true goose at all but more akin to a shelduck, though this does not appear to have affected its social status or lifestyle in any way. It still flies in the best circles and spends a good deal of time on the golf course and is consequently very widespread in South Africa, occurring wherever there are dams, lakes, rivers and country clubs. Unlike most golfers, its diet consists primarily of grass and grain with the odd worm or beetle thrown in.

As far back as the 17th century, Egyptian geese were imported to grace the ornamental lakes and ponds of some of the finest country estates in England, mainly in East Anglia. Small populations have lived there ever since. But hobnobbing with the landed gentry in a far-off land has not been without its problems. The immigrant geese kept their biological clock firmly set to African time and, in consequence, have continued to hatch their chicks in January. Their snooty avian neighbors probably look on in disbelief, given that every swan who's any swan knows this is precisely when nature dials the thermostat down to below zero, and foxes are at their most desperate.

In recent years life has started to change for the better, or for the worse, depending on your point of view. Thanks to global warming, January in Northern Europe is now increasingly survivable for Egyptian goose chicks, and the result has been a population explosion. The species is no longer confined to the gated splendor of English ancestral mansions and has joined the common waterfowl on village ponds in some other parts of Britain. In the 1960s some Egyptian geese made it over the English Channel to settle in the Netherlands, where conditions are much more to their liking, so much so that the breeding population now exceeds that of the UK.

Back home in Africa things haven't been going at all badly either. Large, loud and in your face if you dare to come too close, they are the most commonly encountered waterfowl in South Africa. In some areas, such as the wheat fields of the Western Cape, they have become numerous enough to be regarded as a pest. The birds are usually seen in pairs, but when there is an abundance of food, they often congregate in large numbers, the unruly crowd stomping on as many young shoots as they consume.

Egyptian geese are quarrelsome and bad-tempered by nature and particularly pugnacious in the breeding season. The male bird hisses, and the female honks, which is the one sure way to tell them apart. They are highly intolerant of other birds, including others of their own kind, and think nothing of smashing the eggs of an interloper who has the temerity to try to start a family in their back yard.

On a more positive note, they make exceptionally good parents, bonding for life and defending their brood against all comers, airborne or terrestrial, traditional or high-tech. In a recent incident in the Netherlands, the last picture the nosy pilot of a radio-controlled spy quadcopter saw before his craft crashed to earth was the face of an extremely angry Egyptian goose.

Egyptian geese use a wide variety of nesting sites, often recycling the abandoned nests of other species. They might nest on the ground, in matted vegetation near the water's edge, in a tree hollow or on a cliff ledge. Once in a rare while they choose an artificial structure, such as a ledge at the top of a church tower. This poses no problem when the time comes for the chicks to leave home. The parents stand below and call to them until they've summoned up enough courage to take the leap of faith. Whether by accident or sensible design, the chicks have been known to use drainpipes for the great descent, popping out at the bottom like fluff from a straw, maybe a little stunned but otherwise none the worse for wear.

A pair of Egyptian geese usually produces a clutch of 5–8 eggs, which are incubated exclusively by the female for about four weeks while the male patrols nearby, beak at the ready, looking for trouble. Shortly before they hatch, the mother starts chatting to the eggs, and the chicks in their shells respond. Perhaps they are learning to recite a spell from the Egyptian

Book of the Dead, one meant for gaining access to air and water during the passage through the underworld. It includes the words: "I have guarded the egg of the Great Honker. It is sound, so I am sound. It lives, so I live." And indeed they do, hopefully forever after.

ZEBRA

War and peace, work and play, rain and shine, day and night, the horse has plodded, cantered and galloped its way through most of recorded human history. Until the early part of the 20th century it was present at almost every momentous event that helped shape the world we live in. Bronze statues of noble steeds now stand proudly in public places in most of the world's major cities, inevitably carrying an important bronze somebody or other on their back.

While the horse was building this epic reputation, its close African cousin, the zebra, managed to keep its head down and hence avoided being drawn into bloody battles and interminable parades. There were the odd exceptions. The first zebra to reluctantly reach Europe probably arrived in about AD 240 from a port in North Africa aboard a galley destined for Ostia, the ancient port of Rome. At the end of this dangerous and no doubt uncomfortable journey, the zebra took part in a lavish extravaganza at the Coliseum. It was marveled at and then killed, most probably in an inescapable confrontation with an imported lion.

The Romans came to know the zebra as *hippotigris*, which means "tiger horse" in Latin. The name we use in all likelihood originated in Africa, possibly the Congo, and entered the English language via Portuguese or Spanish during the 1600s. English speakers then liberally applied the word to describe a whole host of other things with black-and-white stripes, from fish to pedestrian crossings.

Being familiar in form and yet strange in appearance, the paradoxical zebra has long been a source of wonder and fascination. Modern scientific theory, based on fetal evidence, maintains that it is a black animal with white stripes, though feel free to argue if you've wagered on the opposite being the case.

This does not, of course, explain why it has such bold and dramatic stripes in the first place, something that seems odd, because it lives in a habitat where all the other animals do their best to blend in. Answering

this puzzling question has become something of a scientific parlor game, and it's now possible to pick from a range of hypotheses, none of them mutually exclusive and all of them far from conclusive.

Early theories proposed that the zebra's stripes are a type of camouflage, helping to conceal the animal in long grass or dazzle and confuse predators when a close-knit group is surprised out in the open. More recently, the stripes have been explained as a way of fooling flies or as a type of air-conditioning, the alternating black and white surfaces absorbing or radiating heat to generate a cooling flow of air around the zebra's body. It may even be that the patterns, each as subtly unique to the animal as a human fingerprint, help them recognize each other, though there is not much in the way of evidence to support that particular theory. If it is true, we are left with the conundrum of how the other uniformly coated quadrupeds tell each other apart.

In any event, zebras don't seem to have completely made up their minds as to whether they like stripes or not, and if they do, whether broad ones or thin ones are more fetching. The quagga, a variant of the plains or Burchell's zebra, appears to have been in the process of losing its stripes altogether, incongruously sporting a pair of dirty white pants when it was hunted to extinction. Heaven knows what that did to upset the air-conditioning system or the fly-fooling apparatus, but it plainly wasn't working well as camouflage.

Cape mountain zebras chose to go in the opposite sartorial direction and have the most complicated and striking stripes of all, particularly on the rump; in consequence, their hides were much favored as ornamental rugs. Thus, in the mid-1960s they, too, came perilously close to extinction.

Despite their close kinship with horses, zebras have always been—and still are—justly compartmentalized in most people's minds with all the other wild and exotic fauna of Africa. However, during the 19th century a few serious attempts were made to domesticate them. This proved to be surprisingly easy, or at least no more difficult than breaking in a horse or a mule. Though not as fleet-footed as the horse, zebras have greater stamina and, at least in the African context, are far more resistant to disease. These attributes appealed in particular to the military, and a few zebras were pressed into service as draft animals and even as mounts for soldiers. More visibly, Sir George Gray, Governor of the Cape Colony in the 1850s, had four zebras trained to pull his carriage and even took them with him when he was posted to New Zealand.

In the end, it was probably the zebra's muscular neck, nervous disposition and vicious kick that saved it from an ignominious life of servitude. Alice Hayes, a well-known horsewoman in the 1890s, recording her ride on a mountain zebra, best sums it up: "The most awkward kicker I ever rode. It was no use trying to rein him back; he had a neck like a bull. He was far too neck-strong to make a pleasant mount for a lady." Well, that's a relief.

CHEETAH

Charlemagne kept a cheetah as a pet and so did Cleopatra, Genghis Khan and Akbar the Great. Akbar reportedly kept 9,000, which seems a bit over the top, even for a 16th-century oriental potentate. In Hollywood during the 1930s it wasn't that weird to see a starlet clattering down the street in her high heels with a cheetah on a lead; it isn't that unusual to see one today in the Gulf states, cruising by in the passenger seat of a Rolls Royce convertible, jewel-studded collar sparkling in the Arabian sun.

As a fashion accessory or a living, breathing symbol of machismo, the cheetah is hard to beat. Of all the big felines they are the only ones prepared to behave even remotely like that ultimate species sellout, the not-so-humble domestic cat. Getting cozy with the human race can have its advantages. There are an estimated 600 million cats curled up on the world's sofas versus about 9,000 wild cheetahs eking out a living in Africa. A mere 100 years ago there were 10 times as many.

Cheetahs have long been flirting with extinction and, according to a current genetic theory, only made it through to modern times by a whisker. That whisker apparently belonged to a single female, the only one left after some unknown catastrophe decimated the species long ago. Not that we should feel particularly smug, genetically speaking. A similar theory holds that the number of human beings once dropped so low that we'd have struggled to make up the numbers for a proper post office queue.

Studies in the Serengeti over the past 30 years have revealed that cheetahs still depend on a few females to hold the line against the devastating infant mortality rate. Try as they might, many mothers just aren't up to the task of protecting and feeding their brood, and many go through their entire lives without successfully raising a single cub. The few supermoms are a caste apart, managing to kill daily and feed their brood in the face of relentless pressure from lions and hyenas. In a few rare instances, they have even been known to take over as foster mothers when a birth mother has been killed or simply given up and walked away.

Cheetahs are justly famous for winning the cup as the fastest mammals on earth, but it may yet prove to be a poisoned chalice. The problem with doing 0–96 kilometers (0-60 miles) per hour in three seconds is that it takes an enormous amount of energy. Not only that, but you have to trim down the bodywork and jettison any idea of carrying heavy weaponry. The result is that the cheetah is a lightweight compared with the other muscle-bound predators that share the same turf. According to people who somehow manage to count such grisly things, lions in the Serengeti kill 95 percent of cheetah cubs. Even the usually obsequious brown hyena sometimes robs them of their kills.

Cheetahs employ different hunting strategies depending upon the terrain. Their traditional method is to lie in wait, making use of cover just like any other cat would, until a suitable target, typically one of the smaller antelope, comes within about 50 or 60 meters (160-200 feet) of it. It then streaks in for the kill, knocking the hind legs out from under its quarry. It may sound easy from the comfort of an armchair, but the antelope is usually no slouch off the mark either. If it can run like the clappers and zigzag three or four times, the cheetah repeatedly overshoots and is soon exhausted. Even when successful, the cat needs to lie down for three or four minutes to get its breath back before feeding, fervently hoping that the freeloaders don't immediately start arriving with their knives and forks.

Despite these hiccups and drawbacks, the cheetahs' system works well in an ideal habitat—well enough to have brought them through from the Pliocene. The problem, of course, is that such habitats are continually shrinking or disappearing altogether. In Asia, they've virtually gone, and the Asiatic cheetah is all but extinct, a handful of highly elusive and gaunt survivors picking their way over the rocky slopes of Iran.

Although relatively easy to train as cubs, cheetahs are neither designed nor inclined to become household pets, unlike their diminutive distant cousins. For their survival now, they are essentially dependent on the wildlife sanctuaries of East and southern Africa, and those, in turn, depend for their existence upon the wisdom and goodwill of a notoriously fickle biped.

GROUND-HORNBILL

The ground-hornbill is regarded as a rain bird in many African cultures, and the consequences of killing one can be dire, not just for the assassin but for the whole community. Goat herder Isidoro Ocak'amani was banned from his village in northern Uganda for 40 years and forfeited his rights of inheritance for slaying one of the birds and thereby causing a prolonged drought that decimated the local economy.

A regional and paradoxical variant of such tribal lore holds that the most effective way to end a drought is to kill one of the birds, recite various incantations and spells and then throw its body into a pool of stagnant water in the local riverbed. The stench is enough to cause the heavens to open and flush away the rotting carcass.

Whether the ground-hornbill, dead or alive, actually has any mystical meteorological influence is impossible for science to determine, but it is perhaps curious to note that the dramatic decline in their numbers has coincided with the onset of climatic shifts in many parts of its present and former range.

Large and prehistoric, with a prodigious predatory bill, the ground-hornbill is a walking advertisement for the increasingly convincing theory that birds are the direct descendants of dinosaurs. It first appeared in the fossil record in the mid-Miocene, some 15 million years ago and, despite the vast passage of time, does not appear to have found it necessary to invest in any significant changes since.

Ground-hornbills are the only habitually terrestrial members of the extensive hornbill family, with the southern ground-hornbill, *Bucorvus leadbeateri*, being the most committed of its genus to a pedestrian lifestyle. Nevertheless, with a wingspan of up to 1.8 meters (6 feet), ground-hornbills are accomplished, if reluctant, fliers and when airborne show their usually concealed white wing feathers to startling effect.

They greet the rising sun with a booming trumpet blast that varies in tone between the sexes. The red throat sac inflates slightly when there's an especially fine sunrise and they feel it important to get out a really good blast. This heraldic duty complete, they set about their daily routine, which consists of walking sedately through woodland or savanna in search of something to eat. They rarely travel alone, usually living in groups consisting of a dominant breeding pair and two or three helpers, although this number can extend up to 10 or 12 individuals of different sexes.

They spread out during their perambulations through the bush, foraging separately but keeping the other members of the party in view, calling to each other if they do get separated. The standard fare consists of insects, lizards, frogs, snails and small rodents, but every now and again they combine to tackle something larger, capturing and killing big snakes, tortoises and small mammals. They particularly favor burnt patches where ready-made and pre-cooked dinners are often available for the undiscerning consumer.

Ground-hornbills are cooperative breeders, with the younger generation undergoing what appears to be a type of apprenticeship, possibly to prepare them for their own parental responsibilities. They nest in a hole in a tree, though given their large size they need to find a substantial one, usually at the base, and sometimes have to make do reluctantly with a crevice in the rocks. For the same reason they skip the usual arboreal hornbill routine of plastering over the nest entrance, sealing the female and her eggs inside and leaving only a sufficient slit to deliver food. This is probably a sensible omission given that the equivalent of half a dozen bags of cement would probably be required to complete the job.

The female lays two eggs and incubates them for about a month, while her partner punctiliously ensures she gets enough to eat, assisted to some degree by other group members. Unlike her walled-up smaller cousins, she

occasionally leaves the nest to stretch her legs and raid the fridge, during which interludes her partner takes over on the nest.

Only one chick usually makes it to maturity, the other inevitably giving up in the contest for food. There is some evidence that the weaker sibling is occasionally killed and even eaten by the parent birds. The lucky survivor spends three months in the nest and is fed by both parents and members of the extended family for a further nine months, a long stretch in avian terms and an investment in time and resources that may explain the instances of infanticide.

The long-lived ground-hornbills are hailed as good investment brokers in African tradition, though this has nothing to do with their forward-looking parental activities. When tribes were on the move and settling new lands, it was considered sound policy to find out where the hornbills routinely spent their time. Such areas were deemed the best land to graze cattle, the established currency and indicator of wealth in many African cultures.

The ever-expanding portfolios of cows, their owners and associated communities do not presage a particularly rosy future for the birds themselves.

DUNG BEETLE

No insect rose to such high eminence in the ancient halls of Egyptian religion as *Scarabaeus sacer*, the sacred scarab. The Egyptians believed that a cosmic scarab, a type of dung beetle, rolled the golden orb of the sun across the sky toward the west during the day and then trundled it through the underworld at night, attending to any necessary repairs and maintenance along the way. When the sun popped up in the east each morning, it was consequently as good as new.

The connection between celestial mechanics and a small beetle rolling a pile of dung about is not so obvious to the modern mind. But before pooh-poohing the idea, it is as well to note that painstaking and excruciatingly precise research has revealed that there is indeed a connection of sorts. Dung beetles apparently manage to roll their ball in a straight line by orienting themselves relative to the sun by day and the Milky Way by night. They need to keep to the straight and narrow in order to make a fast getaway; rolling a dung ball around aimlessly is an open invitation to other beetles to try to steal it, and none of them want that to happen.

Where there's muck there's money, so to speak, and there are hundreds of different species of beetle that make an honest living harvesting dung, as well as a disreputable few who make a habit of stealing it from others. They all prefer it fresh, and the droppings of herbivores and omnivores are especially preferred, having the best mix of nutrients. Hyena droppings, which are hard, white and mainly composed of calcium, can be safely ignored. Elephants provide a colossal bonanza, and an especially large deposit quickly attracts hundreds and sometimes thousands of beetles within a matter of minutes.

Not all dung beetles go through the laborious business of making a ball. Some simply dine al fresco, while others, of the genus *Onitis*, burrow a tunnel into the earth below or very near the dung pile, excavating an ample chamber at the end of it. They then selectively choose the most appetizing items from the steaming pile above with which to stock their larder, just as

185

you would presumably do if a supermarket fell on your head.

The rollers, as they are colloquially known, are thought to have evolved their takeaway method to overcome the intense competition for space one tends to encounter around dung piles, at least if you're a beetle.

The size of the balls some beetles manage to make and then roll away has long amazed observers, and all sorts of bizarre comparisons are made in an attempt to equate the feat to human experience. Suffice it to say that if you ordered a hamburger 10 meters (33 feet) wide and then rolled it a kilometer (0.6 mile) down the street without the lettuce falling out you would not only get into the *Guinness Book of Records* but would also gain some modest insight into what the beetles are up against.

The Egyptians believed that scarab beetles were all male and that they produced offspring by getting intimate with a ball of dung, a bit like a phoenix rising from fire, only not as ostentatiously romantic. Fortunately for the beetles and, let's face it, for the sake of common decency, this is not the case. A female *Scarabaeus* follows the ball-trundling male and waits patiently while he excavates a hole big enough to accommodate the dung. Whether she gives advice such as "surely that goes there" will probably never be determined. When he's finished getting everything just so, she enters the hole to join him for a nuptial feast that can last several days. It may sound a bit gloomy, sans candlelight and a bottle of bubbly, but it's as good a way as any to really get to know one other.

With the feasting over, either the male or the female makes another ball, which the female alone takes down below (and the male leaves). After fairly elaborate preparations she lays a single egg in a hole in the near-perfect sphere, smoothing it over so that her grub will be snug inside and have plenty to eat when it hatches. An added bonus is that the outer layer of the ball will dry out and harden, in effect encasing an egg within an egg. She then departs, filling in the tunnel as she leaves, and scampers off to do it all over again.

Dung beetles are much admired by stock farmers the world over for their incidental propensity to recycle nutrients and aerate the soil, thereby helping to create verdant pastures for cattle and sheep. They are held in particularly high esteem in Australia where beetles imported from South Africa and Europe in the 1980s, presumably as highly skilled immigrants, are credited with a huge reduction in the population of pestilential flies, which are otherwise attracted to dung. A concomitant reduction in the number of Australian stock farmers feeling the need to wear silly hats with corks dangling from their rims has also been recorded. Everyone with even a modicum of fashion sense can be eternally grateful to the beetle for that.

LEATHERBACK TURTLE

An African legend, which varies in the telling but serves to explain the origin of turtles, informs us that a tortoise fled into the sea to avoid an eagle's wrath.

In the story, a king offers his daughter's hand to the first of these two creatures to bring him salt from a distant sea. The race day is set for a month hence, but the tortoise uses the intervening time to plod surreptitiously to the coast, fetch salt and hide it away at the finish line. On the way there and back he persuades other tortoises to position themselves at strategic points along the route on the day of the race so as to be conspicuous to the eagle. Come the appointed day, the two competitors set off, and the eagle is astonished to find that every time he glances down he sees the tortoise apparently more than keeping pace on the ground below. You know who wins. When the deceit is finally discovered, the tortoise flees into the sea where it has been hiding ever since.

This story makes a great deal of sense, excepting of course that it is difficult to understand why the king didn't simply marry his daughter to Prince Charming, like every other monarch in fairy tales.

Sea turtles have almost as many folk tales swirling around them as there are eddies in the ocean. Another popular theme is the mysterious island, replete with sand and palm trees, on which the Ancient Greeks bestowed the name Aspidochelone. Sea-weary mariners who came across this island invariably set up their barbecues only to find—just as the steaks were about ready—that it sank beneath them and was in fact a gigantic turtle.

Chelonia is now the name for the order of reptiles that includes all turtles, tortoises and terrapins, and the biggest of them all is the leatherback turtle. Although not island-sized, unless you're a shrimp, leatherbacks can sometimes reach a carapace length of 1.8 meters (6 feet) and tip the scales at 680 kilograms (1500 pounds). They are further distinguished from other turtles by having a leathery, ridged carapace, as opposed to the hard shells sported by other, smaller species.

Leatherbacks cruise the world's seven seas with consummate ease and do not confine themselves to equatorial waters, ranging as far north as Norway, and southwards beyond the tip of Africa. Their large size and stored fats are assumed to provide a degree of insulation, and they are able to maintain a body temperature higher than the water around them, at least to some extent. This explains why they can function and venture into cold seas, whereas other sea turtles dip a flipper and quickly turn back.

Little was known about the leatherback's movements at sea until the advent of satellite tracking, but even now the trace of their journeys on the world's vast oceans is mostly a blank, like The Bellman's map in Lewis Carroll's *The Hunting of the Snark*. Tagging has at least revealed the remarkable voyages they're capable of, with one individual swimming 6,000 kilometers (3,700 miles) in under 10 months, from the north of South America to Ghana in West Africa, an average of 20 kilometers (12.5 miles) a day, not counting unknown detours.

Leatherbacks apparently know where they're going and where they've been, but what we don't know for certain is how they navigate. The open ocean is a featureless place, and any useful signage on the sea floor is far below and out of reach. Their above-water eyesight is poor, so it is unlikely that the stars in the heavens provide any points of reference, and scents in the restless sea are by the nature of things chaotic and ephemeral. The current thinking is that they navigate using the earth's magnetic field, like some species of birds are believed to do on an overcast day, probably fine-tuning by using other cues as they near their destination.

In the 1970s it was thought that the total number of leatherbacks was dwindling to the point of extinction, but other breeding sites have since been discovered, and some cheerful estimates put the global population as high as 100,000. This may seem a lot but isn't, given the size of the globe and the amount of garbage we dump in the seas every year. Despite their bulk, the leatherbacks eat mainly jellyfish, and our annual contribution to the fauna of the ocean includes tens of millions of plastic bags, which float on or just below the surface and look just like them. If you came back from the shops, tipped your groceries into the bin and instead ate the plastic bag, you'd soon get an idea of the problem this poses.

Male leatherbacks spend their long lives entirely at sea, but individual females come furtively ashore every few years, usually under cover of darkness, to lay their eggs in the sand. One favored site is on South Africa's Maputaland coast where an estimated 500 female leatherbacks emerge from the pounding surf annually and drag themselves laboriously up the beach. Once she's laid her eggs, the turtle transcribes a mystic circle in the sand around her nest, just as the hatchlings will do when they emerge.

Life outside the egg must seem nasty, brutish and short for newly hatched turtles. Everything with a beak, teeth or claws is out to get them, on the beach and in the sea. About 1 percent reach maturity, and only then does nature finally let up and bestow a measure of invulnerability—except of course, from humans.

Although they are protected in most countries, leatherbacks and other turtles are still hunted, particularly along the shores of the Indian Ocean. In Madagascar, poachers believe that they court misfortune if they kill one, but they do it anyway. To propitiate the turtle's spirit they cut off the head and impale it on a stick to face the sea, a home so close but forever out of reach.

BAT

Listing the different types of bat is a bit like the recitation of shrimp recipes in the movie *Forest Gump*. There's the banana bat, the butterfly bat, the fruit bat, the hairy bat, the horseshoe bat, the house bat, the leaf-nosed bat, the long-fingered bat, the slit-faced bat, the woolly bat, and that's more than enough for now. Altogether, there are over 50 species and subspecies of bat hanging out or flapping about in the night skies of southern Africa alone, and the count keeps changing. In the world at large, there are probably well over 1,000, perhaps a quarter of all mammal species.

Science has cajoled bats into two main groups: fruit-eaters, which have large eyes, two claws on each wing and a dog-shaped muzzle; and insectivores, which are generally smaller in size, have smaller eyes, big ears and a single claw on each wing. The insectivores all use echolocation to find their prey, whereas the fruit-eaters, with one exception, use their eyes and noses. All are nocturnal, and many of them roost during the day in the kinds of places and spaces that give us the creeps.

The good news is that none of them has ever heard of Dracula, let alone Gotham City. Despite this forgivable ignorance of popular Western culture, bats have had a bad rap for centuries. Only in recent years has the mood shifted to align more with that of the "inscrutable Orient," where bats, including the flying fox, have always been associated with health, wealth and happiness, particularly in China.

Long before Bram Stoker penned *Dracula*, a babble of fabulous nonsense was believed about bats in medieval Europe. Because they looked vaguely like flying rats, they were assumed to carry disease, but mostly they were associated with witches, warlocks and taking tea with the devil and his demons. Poor old Lady Jacaume of Bayonne in France was burned at the stake in 1332 on incontrovertible evidence that bats had been seen flying about her house and garden. If you're a myopic, sadistic pedant, you don't need any more proof than that.

Stoker simply needed to tap into a rich vein, so to speak, helped

along by a newspaper article he'd read that described how a vampire bat had drained the blood from a child. It would be no mean feat for *Desmodus rotundus,* the common vampire bat, to do that. It weighs only 57 grams (2 ounces). It must have blown up like a rubber balloon and exploded, though the newspaper article in question makes no reference to such a gory postlude.

We need bats more than they need us. According to one estimate, seeds dropped by bats account for most forest regeneration on cleared lands in the Old World tropics. At least 300 plant species are known to be dependent on fruit bats for pollination and seed dispersal, including the fabled baobab tree. Without the sterling services of Wahlberg's epauletted fruit bat, baobabs would likely have become extinct.

If you really want to be impressed, get bats started on mosquitoes and other pestilential insects. South Africa's largest colony comprises the 299,999 bats that live in De Hoop Guano Cave near Bredasdrop in the Western Cape. They are credited with tucking away about 100 tons of insects every year, including many crop pests.

Over in the USA, Mexican free-tailed bats thunder out of large caves in central Texas each night, including the Bracken Caves, which host some 20 million, and chomp their way through about 1,000 tons of insects each and every night. They do things big in Texas. Included in the list of fatalities are millions of corn earworm moths, high up on the USA's Most Not-Wanted list of crop pests.

The lodging householders occasionally provide in return seems miserly in comparison, especially since bats don't spill coffee on the sofa, hog the bathroom or argue about which channel to watch on TV. Bats use a wide variety of natural nesting sites, but all those empty spaces up in the rafters where the water heater quietly runs up whopping bills are pretty much ideal, at least for some species. The vulnerable large-eared free-tailed bat, *Otomops martiensseni*, is confined in South Africa exclusively to roosts in the high-pitched roofs of a few double-story houses in Durban. It needs a good address and a free drop to get airborne, so not every roof will do. These bats don't push their luck as lodgers, forming small colonies of up to a dozen individuals at most, usually females and a single male.

By way of contrast, the super cute banana bat, *Pipistrellus nanus*, though it lives in similarly small groups of fewer than 10 individuals, weighs no more than 4 grams (0.14 ounces) and attains a length of just 80 millimeters (3 inches) at most. Banana bats routinely tuck themselves into the rolled-up terminal leaves of banana plants during the day and pay the rent by emerging at night to feed exclusively on insects.

There isn't much room in a bat's body for the digestive tract, so its diet is restricted to foods that are highly nutritious and easily digestible, be it fruit, nectar or bugs. Virtually all bats are fast feeders and big snoozers, seldom if ever seeing a sunset or a sunrise and dashing about in the dark for only four or five hours a night. They spend the rest of the time, an average of 19 hours a day, roosting under the covers. All animals are vulnerable when they sleep, and sleeping or snoozing as much as they do helps explain why bats seek out the darkest and most inaccessible places to spend the bulk of their largely somnolent lives.

One result is that even in our nosy world of scientific prodding and poking, the lives of most bats are yet little understood, leaving ample room for fear and superstition to flourish. Chiroptophobia (the fear of bats, not of chiropractors) is an especially popular neurosis, and the very idea of a bat getting entangled in our hair is a heartstopper for most of us. Chiropterologists confidently dismiss this as impossible, but it's not always wise to be dogmatic, particularly where bats are concerned. It happened to my mother, sitting in a cloud of mosquitoes on the veranda of a lodge in northern Uganda. The bat survived the entanglement and even provided an excuse, though it was scarcely needed, for a round of double brandies.

BUSHBABY

The tokoloshe is an African creature with nothing whatsoever to recommend it. In appearance, it resembles a little hairy man but is altogether more repulsive and malignant. Its nocturnal habitat is restricted to the borderlands between imagination and hysteria, and in this respect it can be assumed to be related to poltergeists and the other diminutive and imaginary nuisances of different cultures.

From time to time the rare capture and slaying of a tokoloshe is reported in African newspapers, but the corpse invariably and sadly turns out to belong to a galago or bushbaby, an inoffensive little primate whose resemblance to the mythical grotesque is restricted entirely to the coincidental fact that it is small, five-fingered, furry and seldom seen.

Bushbabies are by nature cautious, so much so that they haven't changed much in millions of years and chose to stay behind when the rest of us evolved into monkeys and apes. They even stayed put when Madagascar broke away from Africa and floated off into the Indian Ocean, taking some of their bemused relatives with it. Once the panic had subsided, the Madagascan branch of the family had little option but to make the best of things and evolved into lemurs, which now fill many of the niches occupied by monkeys in Africa and other parts of the world.

When you're cute, small, edible and not very fast it's probably best to stick to the trees, as indeed they do. The lesser bushbaby, *Galago moholi*, is the smaller of the two species that live in southern Africa, typically only weighing about 150 grams (5 ounces)—snack size for a raptor, and a packet of peanuts for anyone else. The greater bushbaby, *Otolemur crassicaudatus*, is a whole lot bigger and sturdier, but still only the size of a small cat. Both have bushy tails that are a lot longer than their bodies and act as stabilizers when they leap between branches. When it comes to jumping, less is more. The greater bushbaby moves more sedately and conventionally than its smaller cousin, which hops rather than walks and can happily clear gaps of 3–4 meters (10-13 feet).

Bushbabies have bulbous and enormous eyes that are fixed in their face like an owl's and sensitive enough to enable them to see by starlight, but they tend to stay put in the same tree on moonless nights, just in case. This has given rise to the accusation that they're afraid of the dark, which seems a bit rich coming from members of a quaking species that has populated the night with all manner of imaginary monsters. Most nights, dangers notwithstanding, they're out and about, even during thunderstorms, foraging within their home range, which varies in size depending on local conditions. It is never very extensive, as most of their modest dietary requirements are close at hand in the forest canopy.

Lesser bushbabies live mainly on gum exuded from holes in trees, the fresher the better, though they vary this chewy staple with the occasional insect snatched from the air or encountered minding its own business on a nearby branch. They can snatch an airborne moth or locust with lightning speed, closing their eyes and averting their face from its flapping wings like a human child being force-fed spinach. Their bigger cousins are also into chewing gum and crunching insects but add supplements in the form of fruit, nectar and seeds.

They routinely use the same arboreal pathways each night, mostly visiting a few familiar trees. They invariably forage alone, and individual territories are marked out in the time-honored manner of urinating in the palm of their cupped hand and then dabbing the concoction on their feet and, when social convention demands it, on each other. The sticky mess has the added bonus of improving their grip. More conventionally, they also use scent glands to stake a claim at strategic points within their branchy domain.

Bushbabies are not especially social creatures, behaving more like a secret society than the gregarious members of a treetop country club. The basic family unit consists of a mother and her offspring of various ages who occupy a urinal home range. Adolescent males are booted out to make their way in the world, the more successful establishing their own territory that overlaps with those of two or three females whom they visit on rotation. The less successful often end up as something's lunch. The territories of dominant males rarely if ever overlap. Social arrangements up in the branches can get very complicated, and this probably explains why bushbabies are so emphatically committed to marking rights of way and boundaries.

They make a variety of vocalizations, depending on their moods and needs, but the distance call of the greater bushbaby is the most singular and arresting, sounding remarkably like a crying human baby. This sound alone is enough to have propelled the diminutive beasts into the realm of magic and superstition, evoking dim and misty recollections of our own beginnings.

CHAMELEON

A number of things differentiate lions and chameleons. Perhaps the most striking is that lions are a lot larger and don't usually try to catch their prey by sticking their tongues out. Nevertheless, the two creatures share a common name, at least in part. An Ancient Greek biologist must have thought the similarities were obvious, because the word chameleon derives from the Greek *chamai*, meaning "on the ground," and *leon*, which means "lion."

Most chameleons are, in fact, mainly arboreal, though as usual there's always someone bucking the trend. The Namaqua chameleon spends most of its time on the ground on the arid and sparsely vegetated plains of Namibia and the sand dunes and bleaker regions of the southwestern parts of South Africa. Though similar in most respects to other chameleons, it can run very well, something it probably has to do quite often, given the lack of decent cover in its chosen habitat.

Nobody is quite sure how many species of chameleon live in southern Africa, although the current count is about 19. The great majority are dwarf chameleons, so called because they're smaller than the others, which are bigger and in the minority. If that nomenclature sounds a bit prejudiced and topsy-turvy, send your complaint in writing to the secretary of your local herpetological society. You may have to wait for a reply as he or she is probably out in the bush all day long trying to work out just how many different types of the little critters there actually are.

It should come as no surprise that new species and subspecies keep popping up, given their ability to blend in and remain practically invisible in trees and bushes by moving about at a bureaucratic pace. Their relative lack of mobility is one factor that is thought to have contributed to the evolution of so many distinct species, each confined to a specific habitat, with little if any overlaps. Some habitats are tiny. The very rare black-headed dwarf chameleon's perilous grip on existence was threatened when a business park was developed in the Cato Manor area of Durban in 2003, which goes to show just how bad things can be.

The most widespread and common species in southern Africa is the flap-neck chameleon, so called because it usually has a hand-me-down collar from a miniature triceratops. Its workaday outfit is emerald green and it's notably less knobbly than other species, many of which have prominent tubercles, crests or spiny ridges running down their backs. The flap-neck is the species most likely to be seen making a dangerous trip across the road in the Kruger National Park. Rather incongruously, its back-and-forth swaying makes it seem as though it's gearing up for a skip and a jump, which despite being physically impossible may well be what it has in mind given the nightmare position it's in.

Some chameleons are more kaleidoscopic than others, but they can all change color to a greater or lesser extent. Changes are not only meant to enhance camouflage, which is good enough in most circumstances, but also to reflect their prevailing mood or to regulate body temperature. When two male Knysna dwarf chameleons meet each other on a branch, the dominant one becomes resplendent in radiant greens and blues, while the wimp tries to look less threatening than a baked potato. The imminent prospect of sex is another stimulus that sees both male and female chameleons rummaging through their wardrobes. The weather also plays a part. They are all diurnal and regulate their body temperature by positioning themselves to expose more or less of their bodies to the sun and, of course, by selecting the right outfit.

The ability to change color is a neat trick, but chameleons aren't the only ones with such skills. Various undersea animals, including the octopus, are capable of more rapid and impressive displays. Perhaps the chameleon's most distinctive features are its extraordinary tongue, which it can shoot out like a party squeaker to a distance equivalent to its body length, and eyes that are capable of operating independently.

The optical control center in a chameleon's brain must be a hectic place. Each beady eye rotates independently through 180 degrees, scanning the surroundings for potential meals and threats. When one side spots something, the head turns in that direction so that the other eye can join in, rather like swapping a telescope for a pair of range-finding binoculars. Cerebral pandemonium must break out if one eye spots a threat and the other a meal at exactly the same moment. Rather than take out the condiments and place mats, in such circumstances it's probably best to turn green and sway like a leaf, something chameleons do very well.

Although various mammals, including monkeys, are an ever-present threat, chameleons are mainly preyed upon by snakes and birds. Fiscal shrikes have the nasty habit of impaling small chameleons on acacia thorns, a prospect marginally more ghastly than being caught napping and swallowed whole by an arboreal boomslang. With such unpleasant prospects in mind, and knowing that birds and snakes see the world differently, some chameleons seem able to tailor their camouflage specifically to counter threats from these principal predators.

In an increasingly frantic world and despite the dangers they constantly face, chameleons are determined not to be hurried and choose instead to live in a self-imposed oasis of calm. Living a generally languorous life is perhaps one thing they do, after all, have in common with lions.

MONITOR LIZARD

The earliest recorded instance of a monitor lizard being kept as a pet comes to us in the form of a story from the borderlands of India and Bangladesh.

Dawa, the founder of a clan of the Garo tribe, captured a baby water monitor and put it in a cage. On each of the days that followed, the lizard's concerned parents came to visit their imprisoned offspring. Astonished by their enormous size, Dawa grew increasingly worried they would take revenge. He finally released the young monitor, gave it a yellow coat and a set of earrings, and promised the parents that he would never capture one again. In return they promised not to harm him or his family. In a postscript, we learn that Dawa and the young monitor became firm friends and when the lizard grew up it often carried him across the river on its back.

Recent developments in Palm Beach County in the State of Florida do not seem set for such a happy outcome. *Varanus niloticus*, the Nile or water monitor, imported into Florida from Africa by dealers in exotic pets, have found their way out of cages and condos and into a habitat very much to their liking. Included on their New World grocery list are domestic cats, a sensitive food choice that has led to violent confrontations between the reptiles and gun-toting local law enforcement, not to mention creating angst among the bejeweled retirees of Palm Beach County.

Explaining why anyone would want a Nile monitor as a domestic pet is a conundrum best left to professionals. Like most species they're cute when they're small, but they grow up to be the biggest lizards that Africa has to offer. An adult has jaws like a steel trap, claws capable of slicing your arm to the bone and a muscular tail it can swing like a baseball bat.

Monitors are more closely related to snakes than to lizards and have the forked tongue and the venom to prove it, albeit in doses too small to be lethal to humans. But not to worry, they may also have a mouth full of salmonella, streptococcus and a host of other bacteria to make up for the deficiency. To top it off, they don't like people or anything else for that matter, including each other most of the time. Even their nuptials are fraught with dangers. If you want to kiss and cuddle a Nile monitor you had best be prepared for a medical emergency.

Monitors purportedly got their name because of a mix-up in translation between Arabic and German, but the general consensus is that they're named for their habit of watchfulness; they seem to continually monitor their surroundings for dangers and opportunities. The Ancient Egyptians would probably have concurred. They apparently tethered monitors to the banks of the Nile as a kind of crocodile early-warning system. If the lizard remained placid, it was safe to swim, but if it became agitated it was taken as a sign that a crocodile was lurking nearby. Dutch explorers thought they looked like iguanas and they hence became known as *leguan* in Afrikaans.

There are about 78 known species of monitor lizard in the world and by far and away the largest is the Komodo dragon, which lives on various islands in Indonesia and eats water buffalo. Let me quickly add that, big as it is, the Komodo doesn't swallow them whole. It dashes in and inflicts a bite that invariably causes an infection so virulent that the hapless buffalo keels over in a couple of days. The humongous lizard then feeds at its leisure.

Africa is home to two species, the water monitor and the rock monitor, *Varanus albigularis*, which is a little smaller than its closely related cousin. As their names suggest, they occupy different habitats. The water monitor lives in close proximity to rivers, swamps, lakes and pools, as well as along the seashore throughout Africa, while its cousin favors the bush, feeling particularly at home in rocky terrain. Both species are accomplished tree climbers and spend a good deal of time basking on branches. A water monitor often chooses a branch overhanging a riverbank so that it can drop straight into the water if it has to, or into a canoe being paddled quietly along underneath, as was reported in one alarming case.

Water monitors are solitary creatures, but they sometimes cooperate to steal eggs from a crocodile's riverbank nest. One lizard pulls reptilian faces at the croc and, when the offended monster indignantly lunges after it, the other darts in behind, digs like crazy and helps itself. They then purportedly swap roles. A type of plover, appropriately and colloquially known as a *dikkop* or thickhead, is known to lay its eggs on the ground close to a crocodile's nest, presumably in the hope that the brooding crocodile will be uninterested in the bird's modest clutch and scare off any possible predators simply by being there and looking ferocious. We can assume that the canny water monitors thus also get to enjoy an occasional side dish.

When it comes to laying their own eggs, water monitors take sensible precautions. They look for an active termite mound and, if one is available, break a hole in the wall and deposit their eggs inside. For some reason, the termites don't attack the clutch and instead set about repairing the damage, thereby sealing up the eggs in a safe, humid and temperature-controlled environment.

The young can take up to a year to hatch. When they do, they make their way through the termite's air-conditioning ducts like burglars leaving a heist, probably snacking on termite guards along the way. There has been speculation that the mother returns to free the hatchlings, but this would presuppose an uncanny sense of timing, let alone a remarkable memory. Like her rock monitor cousin, who simply buries her eggs in a hole, she probably forgets all about them.

Monitor lizards play different roles in the folklore of disparate peoples, varying from benign to evil. In Borneo, if a monitor lizard comes between two warring tribes they call off the battle, and that can only be good. In parts of Pakistan it's best to keep your mouth firmly shut if you encounter a monitor; if it sees your teeth it can somehow steal your soul.

Some believe that monitors' flicking tongues gave rise to the idea of fire-breathing dragons, mythical creatures that themselves have enigmatic and contrary reputations. Although there are other credible candidates for that distinction, monitors do have an otherworldly look about them. The monitor was the first animal to come ashore 40 years after the devastating volcanic eruption of Krakatau, easing itself up out of the waves onto the primordial and sterile cinders. What drew it to such a wasteland, nobody knows. It can't possibly have mistaken it for Palm Beach.

GIRAFFE

If the giraffe didn't exist we probably couldn't invent it. The Ancient Greeks, who were always up for an intellectual challenge, nevertheless gave it a try. They had to rely on Egyptian travelers' tall tales, because they'd never laid eyes on a live one. The result was a cross between a camel and a leopard. Even in a daydream that sounds like a biological and mechanical impossibility, so they consigned their hybrid to the realm of myth.

The Egyptians knew better. Ramses II had one in his menagerie, a prize possession somehow transported down the Nile from the East African savanna. Giraffes are by nature nosy parkers, better adapted to seeing over the heads of the crowd than any other animal, so the pharaoh's delightful and unusual pet probably found the sights and sounds of Giza fascinating.

Giraffes were eventually introduced to Europe via circuses, zoos and private collections and, although always rare, settled into the ordinary European mind as bizarre but nevertheless real rather than imaginary creatures.

A problem arose when Charles Darwin returned from his trip on the *Beagle*, clutching copious notes and boxes of samples and then sat down and wrote *On the Origin of Species*. The book went through several editions and in the sixth one Darwin decided to tackle the giraffe. Not everyone had found his theory of evolution credible, and his opponents seized on the one-of-a-kind giraffe as a glaring example to argue that evolution was codswallop. Darwin maintained that the giraffe had evolved to feed from the tops of trees and wrote: "By this process long-continued, which exactly corresponds with what I have called unconscious selection by man, combined no doubt in a most important manner with the inherited effects of the increased use of parts, it seems to me almost certain that an ordinary hoofed quadruped might be converted into a giraffe." So began a verbose debate that still rages to this day.

The problem with giraffes is that they have no close living relatives and are so radically different from everything else. Even the fossil record hasn't turned up much in the way of clues. Evolutionists breathed a sigh of relief when the okapi, sporting a zebra's bum and a long neck, emerged from the Congo forest to astonish the world in 1901. The okapi was quickly bundled into the same family as the giraffe, but not everyone's convinced.

Giraffes, and for that matter okapis, don't always abide by the evolutionary rules laid out for having such an extraordinary neck. For a start, female giraffes are on average about a meter (3 feet) shorter than males. The young, of course, are even shorter, and either they're getting the short end of the stick, so to speak, or neck length doesn't matter as far as survival is concerned. It has also been pointed out that giraffes don't always, or even usually, eat from the tops of trees anyway. Females frequently eat with their necks almost horizontal. Only the big bulls routinely stretch up for the presumably delectable leaves at the tippy top and in the process lose sight of what's going on down below. This may partly explain why nearly twice as many male giraffes as females fall victim to lions.

With their compelling urge to have a unique perspective on what the neighbors are up to, giraffes seem to have done some kind of private deal with nature. Being on stilts has its downside, of course, not least when they want to drink. When that happens they need to lower their head through 4.5 or 5 meters (15-16.5 feet) and then whip it back up again every few seconds to check that there isn't anything sneaking up on them. That would be enough to make anyone dizzy, but giraffes cope with the problem by having a unique circulatory system. Their hearts beat 150 times a minute, and a complicated system of valves, overflows and elastic artery walls ensures enough blood stays in the brain to prevent them from seeing stars and keeling over.

Nature drew the line at providing parachutes, and a newborn giraffe consequently has to drop into the world with a bit of a bump. Like the young of most species, they're fortunately tougher than they look and in a matter of seconds work out that all those wobbly and bendy poles on what must be their bottom half are actually legs. They're up soon enough, already 1.8 meters (6 feet) tall and able to totter after Mom as she moves off to check out what everyone else has been up to in her absence.

Young giraffes are weaned at about seven months and stay with their mothers for two or three years. The other adults do their own thing, drifting together and then moving apart in a constant shuffling of the groups within each local community. They don't seem to want to miss out on any gossip, but they also like their space and rarely bunch up in the manner of other ungulates.

Mature bulls are prone to wander on their own, though they seldom miss an opportunity to poke their nose into a passing female's business to check whether she's ready for a bit of slap and tickle. Young males are more likely to hang out together, indulging in occasional neck-wrestling matches to establish or maintain a dominance hierarchy, something that's usually more or less sorted out early on in the life of their given community.

Only when a large bull wanders in over the horizon do things get hectic. The local dominant bull and the interloper square up, standing side by side and use their heads to wallop each other's bellies and flanks with pendulum blows. Such choreographed battles are very seldom fatal, but the sound of each impact can be heard a good distance away, not infrequently attracting the attention of lions that then amble over with their own agenda. Lions are a perennial pain in the neck as far as giraffes are concerned, but a problem that comes with the territory.

While returning the stare of a giraffe, it's easy to imagine it'd be amused if it knew of the controversy that rages around the question of how and why giraffes got to be as they are. Despite their imposing height, they don't look down their noses, and their expression never seems arrogant or superior. Their soulful eyes and charming demeanor suggest instead a kind of benevolent curiosity, as befits one of the world's most curious creatures.

FLAMINGO

When considering the flamingo, it's difficult to decide whether nature was cracking a joke or showing off. How a bird that apparently shares its ancestry with the diminutive grebe could be persuaded to get up on stilts, turn its beak upside down and equip itself for a gay parade is one of life's enduring puzzles. Flamingos are ungainly and yet elegant, garish and yet gorgeous; they can raise a laugh or reignite the smoldering souls of poets. It comes as no surprise that Lewis Carroll chose to employ them as croquet mallets in the illogically logical world of *Alice in Wonderland*.

There are six extant species of flamingo, and they are all, by and large, cut from the same colorful cloth and follow the same basic design. A seventh type, Featherstone's flamingo, is differentiated by the fact that it's made of plastic. It can be found on manicured lawns in suburban America, usually singly or in pairs but sometimes in flocks. Originally created in 1957 by Don Featherstone for the garden ornament company Union Products, the current population of indestructible pink plastic flamingos is estimated to run into millions. While reviled by many as the pinnacle of kitsch, the Smithsonian recognizes the enigma as an icon of American folk art, and in 2009 it was adopted, believe it or not, as the official plastic bird of the City of Madison in the State of Wisconsin.

Real flamingos are not endemic to the USA, least of all Wisconsin, and traditionally favor tropical and subtropical climes. The closest naturally occurring populations of American flamingos, *Phoenicopterus ruber*, are found on islands in the Caribbean. Three other New World species live further south, notably in Chile. The exotic and appealing vision of paradise that the birds conjure up in the jaded minds of commuting America probably explains the enduring appeal of Mr. Featherstone's immobile replicas.

The world's most widespread living and breathing species is the greater flamingo, *Phoenicopterus roseus*, which occurs in isolated communities in many parts of Africa, southern Europe and southeast Asia. The most numerous is the lesser flamingo, *Phoeniconaias minor*, particularly famous for gathering in vast flocks, numbering in the tens of thousands, on the inhospitable soda lakes of East Africa's Great Rift Valley. Where they overlap, including in South Africa, the two species are sometimes found together, sharing the same habitat.

Both species are filter feeders but largely target different prey and so have no reason to get testy with each other. The lesser flamingo feeds mainly on plankton and algae, while the bigger bird tucks into small aquatic invertebrates, insects and tiny fish, but their method of feeding is essentially the same. They dip their bristle-lined topsy-turvy bill into the water and sweep it to and fro like a sieve. Their tongue acts like a piston to pump out the water, and the bird then swallows the mush. Baby flamingos are born with light gray plumage and the pinks and reds of adult birds are derived mainly from the carotene and bacteria in their diet. Generally speaking, the pinker the flamingo the better it's fed and the happier it probably feels.

All flamingo species are gregarious, which is just as well, because nature has been remarkably stingy in providing habitats to meet their preferred feeding, breeding and security requirements. The ideal combination sometimes leads them to places that most other birds, animals and even most fish would regard as hell on earth. Soda lakes, like those in the Great Rift Valley, typically have few, if any, large fish to compete for the organisms the birds feed on. The catch is that such lakes often have no

outlet, and if the inflow of fresh water drops, the salts remorselessly build up. At the best of times the birds have to visit nearby streams regularly to clean their plumage. In bad years the saline balance can get so out of kilter that it dooms the chicks. Salt gradually builds up on their legs, eventually forming heavy manacles that make walking difficult and the prospect of flying impossible.

Aside from such gloomy natural traps, things usually work out, and the birds are capable of staging some of the biggest and most flamboyant parties on the planet. Their en masse synchronized mating rituals can be hilarious to our eyes, though they'd probably be mortified to hear it. But they've got the moves, baby, easily outshining a heaving mass of self-conscious teenage disco dancers.

The point of these synchronized displays is to pair off and get everyone in the mood. Once the fun's over they get down to the serious business of nest building. The result is a mini-volcano made mainly of mud. The female lays a single egg in the caldera, and the parents take turns sitting on the nest. Both parents feed the chick for several weeks with crop milk manufactured by glands in their upper digestive tract; they are among the few birds to have evolved such an intimate method.

Flamingo chicks instinctively know that they're one of a crowd rather than one of a kind, congregating into small neighborhood crèches within two weeks of hatching. Where there's a large population, these small crèches gradually coalesce into a super-group containing all the chicks in the colony. The purpose, of course, is to counter the threat from predators, but fish eagles, jackals and hyenas like to pop in now and again to point out the deficiencies.

A flamingo chick can potentially look forward to a remarkably long life, although there are no guarantees in the wild. A male greater flamingo that arrived in the Adelaide Zoo in Australia in 1933 finally died in 2014, at the ripe old age of 83. At the time, he was the oldest creature in the zoo, a martyr to arthritis. His sole companion over many years was an Andean flamingo that, at a sprightly 65, still soldiers on alone.

FISH EAGLE

Eagles used to be regarded as messengers of the gods and still are in some cultures, including in Africa. In South America, the Aztec god Huitzilopochtli despatched an eagle to help with the site plan for Tenochtitlan, their capital city. The bird sat on a cactus and ate a snake, and that was apparently more than enough inspiration for city engineers. On the other side of the Atlantic, Zeus sent an eagle from Olympus to kidnap Ganymede, a Greek shepherd boy, apparently because the lad was easy on the eye, and the god thought he'd make a good drinks waiter, among other things.

Nowadays eagles have better ways to spend their time than carrying notes and running errands for the gods, the import of which are invariably ambiguous and at worst downright sinister. The birds nevertheless continue to soar through the human psyche as symbols of the mystic, military and majestic. They have led Roman legions into battle and down through the ages have been represented on innumerable flags and standards, wings outstretched, grasping all manner of military symbols and paraphernalia in their talons.

The African fish eagle features in the coat of arms of no fewer than three African countries, two in the south and one in the north, giving a rough idea of the bird's extensive distribution. Its image is evoked in countless commercial contexts, peddling everything from luxury tourist lodges to spare tires. For many, the distinctive call of the fish eagle is the sound that most evokes Africa, even beating out a lion's roar, if only by a whisker.

Not bad for a kleptoparasite. Despite their regal status, African fish eagles clearly don't feel constrained by the notion of noblesse oblige and make a regular habit of robbing other fish-eating birds of their catch. Among their nonplussed victims are pied kingfishers, Goliath herons and saddle-billed storks. Their thieving proclivities don't end there. They have been known to steal prey from other raptors, including the odd snake from a martial eagle.

Fish eagles are also partial to the plump waterfowl that share their domain. Species that need to keep a particular lookout for an unwelcome, and often fatal, royal visit include coots, grebes and ducks, but the list of potential victims, avian and otherwise, is virtually endless. On the salt lakes of East Africa's Rift Valley, fish eagles often dine on flamingos, both chicks and adults, recalling the banquets of Imperial Rome where platters of flamingo tongues were a regular item on the emperor's table.

Day-to-day fare is more humdrum and plebeian. Depending on the locale, the bulk of a fish eagle's diet consists of fish, which it catches itself. As we can expect of a bird that Hollywood would struggle to invent, the eagle accomplishes this routine task with majestic aplomb. Descending from on high in a shallow dive, it seems to tear a slit in the still, golden surface of the water with its talons and effortlessly extract a silver and slippery prize. Well, that's what the script says. Sometimes it works, and at other times the bird grabs hold of a glutinous mullet or a catfish that has never heard of Weight Watchers. About 2 kilograms (4.5 pounds) is the upper limit for an aerial lift; above that and the bird resorts to rushing the fish along the surface to the nearest bank. Even heavier and it has to struggle ignominiously to shore with its tubby catch using its wings as paddles. It doesn't always have a choice. It's sometimes stuck to its lunch, because its feet are lined with small barbs, whose function is to prevent prey from slipping away.

Although widespread in Africa, fish eagles are restricted by their basic needs to the vicinity of large lakes and dams, estuaries and the banks of perennial rivers. Immature birds are an exception. Rather like adventurous backpackers, they often pop up where they're least expected, perhaps choosing to see more of the world but more likely driven out by bossy adults. The greatest concentrations of breeding pairs occur in Botswana's Okavango Delta and in the Great Lakes region of East Africa. South Africa, with its relative dearth of large rivers and lakes, has a small population, estimated to number no more than 500 pairs.

Fish eagles are monogamous and highly territorial, usually establishing their throne at the top of a tall tree as near as possible to the water's edge. On the huge artificial lake of Kariba, between Zambia and Zimbabwe, they occasionally opt for a moat and build their nest on a dead tree standing in the water. A pair of birds may have two or more waterfront properties within their territory, which they use in rotation, but more often than not they stick to a single one, refurbishing it with reeds, grass, twigs and crowns of papyrus, as needs be. It's not particularly capacious, certainly not what you'd call a palace, unless you're a pigeon, but the view is always second to none. Barring coups and accidents they occupy this aerie for the duration of their reign, which can span up to 24 years, just short of a silver jubilee.

The female usually lays two eggs, and the chicks hatch within a couple of days of each other. As befits their rank in the food chain, fish eagles are beneficent providers, and both chicks, sometimes three, are invariably fledged. The chicks do fight in the nest, especially in the early days, but the younger bird generally holds its own, and as they grow the squabbles peter out.

Both sexes utter the bird's famous call, throwing their heads back over their shoulders as though their message is meant for the gods in the skies above, as well as mere mortals. If the gods deign to reply, the eagles now keep the answer to themselves.

BLACK-BACKED JACKAL

The jackal-headed god Anubis played a pivotal role in the funerary rights of Ancient Egypt. He monitored the Scales of Truth to protect the dead from eternal death and conducted the Opening of the Mouth ceremony, among other important official duties. Anubis probably got the job by association, because jackals were always hanging around Egyptian burial grounds. This suggests that visibility and persistence can get you deified or at least elected to high office, even if you have a thin CV and dubious motives.

To be fair, jackals didn't actually apply for a job in the Egyptian pantheon, but they have always been granted the capacity for cunning. In African folk tales they are usually portrayed as tricksters who exploit the gullibility of other supposedly lovable and affable creatures. Such stories invariably end with the dimwit hero outwitting the jackal, an outcome that tends to disappoint cynics and leave lingering doubts about the efficacy of natural justice.

Having a name synonymous with treachery and deceit in popular culture is bad enough, but jackals have slid even further down the slippery slope of opprobrium. They are still regarded by some as vermin and hunted or poisoned in many areas of southern Africa, in effect becoming victims of their own success. Jackals live on their wits, something that has enabled them to survive, and even flourish, in areas outside game reserves, where other large carnivores were long ago exterminated to make way for sheep and people. The latter includes those folks who've still got plenty of bullets left over from killing the last lion.

Black-backed jackals are omnivorous, and, like most of us, they certainly enjoy lamb chops. Given the opportunity, they will prey on accessible livestock, especially those that are weak or incapacitated. However, by far the bulk of their diet consists of wild fare. Typical menus include lizards, insects, rodents, small mammals and even items as large as impala and juvenile wildebeest, the latter brought down in rarely witnessed cooperative hunts. They also chew grass to aid digestion and eat fruit and berries to the extent that the jackal-berry, a fruit-bearing tree, is named after them.

In game reserves where major carnivores are thankfully still alive and able to attend to their daily business, black-backed jackals are probably best known as highly nimble and opportunistic camp followers. They frequently shadow lions, hyenas and even the diminutive honey badger in anticipation of a free meal. They don't always wait at a kill until the formal diners have retired for brandy and cigars, being prepared to take the occasional big risk by darting in to snatch a morsel from within inches of a lion's massive paws, a liberty they don't usually take with leopards or cheetahs.

Despite their widespread distribution and familiarity, not a great deal is known about the black-backed jackal's social life beyond their immediate family. They've kept that largely under wraps, possibly because they're worried about the defamatory distortions we might come up with. They do drop the occasional enigmatic clue that things are not always as simple as they may appear. While they're usually seen alone or as a couple, jackals nevertheless exhibit some hierarchical and social behaviors normally associated with pack animals, including elaborate rituals of dominance and submission. Large groups can assemble out of nowhere to mob a predator or to take advantage of unusual bounty, responding to a vocal code we've yet to crack. There is even some anecdotal evidence that they share information about places to avoid.

Their family life is better understood. A female black-backed jackal selects a mate from several suitors, and the pair then settles into a monogamous relationship that will normally last the rest of their lives. They both work hard to establish and maintain a territory—which varies in extent depending on seasonal and local conditions—by regularly using urine and feces to define the border. Chasing out other home-hunting couples who don't read the signs or pretend they don't smell them is an irritating and ongoing chore. News soon gets around if one of the pair dies, and, with scant displays of sympathy, the survivor is chased off the property to make way for a new couple. Callous as this may seem, at the best of times desirable homes are in short supply, a problem familiar to young newlyweds the world over.

Three or four cubs, sometimes fewer or more, are born in early spring in an underground den, more often than not provided by an aardvark. The family may use two or three dens on their property when raising a family. The mother decides when it's time to move, and pops just has to go along with it, whether he sees the point or not. Even when they're only a few weeks old, the pups aren't carried by the scruff of the neck; instead mom entices them along with false promises of milk. It gets the job done and at the same time imparts a devious lesson taken straight from the jackal's practical book of life.

Young jackals share their parents' territory, gradually roaming further afield until they find a mate and then get to join the housing queue. While they're still around they help with rearing the next litter, contributing food and acting as babysitters. For reasons best known to jackals themselves, pups are born in the leanest season, and the extra help can make a big difference, with some studies suggesting that the number of helpers is directly related to the number of pups that make it to maturity.

Jackals are among the earliest and oldest members of the *Canis* genus, and they've had a long time to size us up. Excavations at a Stone Age human site in South Africa's Western Cape turned up fossil bones that were assumed to be those of dogs but on analysis proved to belong to a black-backed jackal. This find gives a tantalizing hint that a semi-domestic arrangement of sorts may once have existed between our early forebears and the jackal. If it did, it didn't last. There is no evidence that dogs and jackals have ever interbred or that the black-backed jackal has ever been truly domesticated. Perhaps, like Anubis, they weighed us on the Scales of Truth and decided that we're not, after all, to be trusted.

OSTRICH

At some point in its evolutionary history, probably after the dinosaurs had punched out, the ostrich must have decided that the latest set of predators was a bunch of wimps. Rather than continuing to expend energy taking to the air in every minor emergency, it made up its mind to stick to the ground, grow enormous and have a crack at the bipedal land-speed record.

For a long time this kind of crazy explanation just didn't make sense to us. As a species, we've been dreaming about getting airborne since the days of Icarus and probably long before that. Even the odd australopithecine probably thought he'd finally worked it out, flapped his hairy arms and ended up as a squidgy mess at the bottom of a cliff. So who in their right mind would give up the ability to fly, if they had it? In consequence, it was long believed that ostriches had always been earthbound plodders. They had the right idea, even had the feathers, but otherwise never quite got their act together.

Recent DNA research seems finally to have proved that the ostrich's ancestors did hand back their pilots' licenses after all. So did the forebears of the emu, cassowary and all the other flightless birds. It was a daring thing to do. Nature can get mighty ticked off if you return one of her gifts and it didn't work out for everyone. The elephant bird of Madagascar and the giant moa of New Zealand, both bigger than the ostrich, will not, alas, be joining us for lunch. But the ostrich, though never an avian Einstein, seems to have had a better plan.

The land-speed record for bipeds turned out to be a bit of breeze, 70 kilometers (43.5 miles) per hour with the top down. In theory, an ostrich can kiss goodbye to nearly all terrestrial predators except the cheetah. It can see them a mile away, no problem, because it is anything up to 2.7 meters (9 feet) tall and has eyes as big as its brain. Granted, operating such state-of-the-art optics takes up a sizeable chunk of its cerebral capacity, more than half by some estimates, so while the remaining synapses struggle to keep

up, the ostrich is sometimes inclined to get a bit flustered and run around in circles. But if it inadvertently ends up running toward a predator instead of away from it, that's still not the end of the world. It has also evolved a kick that any rugby fly-half would sell his mother to possess, and feet with formidable single claws capable of disemboweling just about anything that tries to eat it.

Many folks in the Arab world think they're the dumbest bird they've ever come across and—let's not beat about the bush—nobody else has ever had particularly high expectations. Anything that swallows the kind of stuff an ostrich does must surely be a dumbass. The point in swallowing pebbles is to help with digestion, the kind of thing crocodiles do without ill effects. But ostriches tend to get carried away or distracted, at least in captivity, and gobble up all sorts of farmyard detritus. Having an elastic throat is all very well, but it doesn't mean that spark plugs, tin cans, bits of old rope and all kinds of other rubbish can be usefully passed down as grist to the mill. More than one ostrich autopsy has had veterinarians shaking their heads in disbelief. But we all have our quirks. Some of us, even the brainiest, routinely swallow copious amounts of slickly packaged ethanol, much to the astonishment and consternation of our livers.

Pliny the Elder was responsible for the most enduring and popular libel, claiming that ostriches hid their heads in the sand at the first sign of trouble. The point, he explained, was that the bird was stupid enough to believe that if it couldn't see anything, nothing could see it. Aristotle disagreed, but then again he had more or less made up his mind that the ostrich was some sort of avian-mammal hybrid, because it had eyelashes and a hairy neck. He wasn't entirely wrong. Unlike other birds, ostriches have indeed evolved some other mammal-like features: they urinate and defecate separately, as opposed to letting fly the splat that hits your car when you've just finished washing it. They've also been busy with modifications to their reproductive apparatus. If you want to hear more about that, write in and I'll send you the details in a plain wrapper.

Ostriches are prolific breeders; a female is capable of laying up to 100 gigantic eggs each year. Where circumstances dictate they're monogamous, but if his luck's in, a male can lord it over a harem of several females. Either way it's his job to build the nest. Clambering into a tree is out of the question, so the nest ends up being a nondescript scrape in the ground. The dominant female lays the first egg, and the others, if there are any, follow. They can eventually assemble a clutch of up to 20 eggs. The leading lady sneaks back every now and again to make sure her eggs stay in the middle, presumably on the assumption that any predator will go for the outer ones first.

It was a common belief in the Middle Ages that ostriches incubate their eggs by staring at them, the heat of their gaze being quite sufficient. In reality they employ the conventional method. The hen, with her drab brown feathers, takes the day shift, and the male takes over in his black outfit during the night. It takes a biblical 40 days and 40 nights for the eggs to hatch. Pneumatic drills or pickaxes are not provided, so the chicks take two days to finally peck their way out of their colossal shells, not surprisingly emerging puffed and soaking wet.

We are all bound by the consequences of our ancestors' decisions and when born have little choice but to accept the world as we find it. Perhaps it's just as well that ostriches don't have the kind of brain that feeds the soul with doubt and introspection. If they did, chicks hiding from a raptor circling in the sky above would surely look to their own feathers and wonder why they'll never leave the earth and fly.

FUR SEAL

According to Celtic legend, selkies are beings who live in the seas around Orkney and other remote isles to the north of Britain. They are indistinguishable from seals, but once ashore they shed their seal skins and take on human form. They are invariably gentle, wise and beautiful. If an islander meets a female selkie on the beach and succeeds in stealing and hiding her seal-skin coat, she is obliged to remain with him as a loyal wife and bear him children, though she will always pine for the sea.

The legend betrays something of the loneliness of island life and also touches upon the curiously precarious status of seals. Unlike whales and dolphins, which evolved to give birth to their young at sea, seals were still hedging their bets in the Miocene. *Puijila darwini*, a fossil creature recently unearthed in Canada, has been hailed by science as the missing link in the evolution of seals, but it still had legs; it was equally adept at getting about on land as in the water, rather like an otter. The decision to opt for flippers must have come later, but even then the tricky issues relating to procreation were deferred for future generations.

Modern seals are now stuck between the sea and a hard place during the breeding season and could be forgiven for wondering whether their distant forebears had adequately thought things through. Flippers may allow seals to do as they please in the sea, but they're a bit of a flop when it comes to getting about on land. And pups are especially vulnerable on shore, even in the most desolate places, easily falling victim to land-based predators, like jackals and hyenas. Nevertheless, with a robust birth rate, these drawbacks were not a decisive issue until commercial hunters came along.

The first mariners to arrive at the Cape of Good Hope were mighty impressed by the "unspeakable numbers" of seals they encountered, and over the years they did their best to address the situation. Their success can be measured by the fact that no populations of fur seals of practical use remained at the Cape when Jan van Riebeeck merrily stepped ashore in 1652. Undeterred, and ever with an eye on profit, Van Riebeeck promptly despatched the yacht *Goede Hoop* to Saldanha Bay to look for more. It soon returned with 2,700 pelts abandoned by French sealers who had clubbed so many that they couldn't find room for the discarded stock aboard their own ship.

Europeans had certainly had sufficient practice in seal clubbing by the time they reached the Fairest Cape. Starting in the years of the Roman Empire, Mediterranean monk seals were nudged ever closer to extinction by regular massacres, a relatively minor rehearsal for what was to follow around the world. Clubbing reached a frenetic pitch in the late 17th and the first half of the 18th centuries, when seals of all species were killed en masse for their pelts, meat and oil. The record was set by the captain and crew of the *Seringapatam*, which returned to London from the South Pacific island of Más a Tierra in 1801, its timbers groaning under the weight of 1 million pelts. The island, now renamed Isla Róbinson Crusoe, had been the castaway home of Andrew Selkirk, the real-life inspiration for Daniel Defoe's practical and innovative hero. This incidental fact demonstrates that even extreme isolation provided seals with little protection.

With an eye on tourism and their ears pinned back by the conservation lobby, governments now ban or tightly control seal hunting. Populations have recovered in some areas to the extent that seals are once again facing the age-old accusation of theft from the fishing industry, a global enterprise now beleaguered by the consequences of its own efficiency.

Like their counterparts around the world, Cape fur seals certainly eat plenty of fish; that's why their kind headed for the sea in the first place. In particular, they need to bulk up in time for the breeding season, the heftier the better. Big bulls get the prime seafront properties, and that's where the ladies like to be. If a bull arrives late or doesn't fancy squaring up to a 200-kilogram (440 pounds) mountain of belligerent lard, he ends up in a modest estate on the rocks or at the back of the beach. With no view and restricted access to the sea, his bleak patch doesn't merit a second glance when the highly pregnant ladies waddle ashore. If that happens, the best plan is to forget about sex and go fishing, which is exactly what most young bachelors do.

Being around as a spectator for the unedifying squabbles between pregnant females probably isn't such a great idea anyway. Fights over the best spot within a male's desirable territory can be vicious, so much so that the resident bull sometimes has to heave himself up off the sofa and come over to help sort things out. Everyone eventually settles down, but the bull still has his work cut out, moving his substantial paunch between upwards of a couple of dozen moody females on his property to check they have everything they need. In between, he bellows at any neighbor who has the temerity to put a flipper over the property line. The mayhem goes on for six weeks, and he never has time for a sardine sandwich, let alone a proper lunch.

Females give birth within a few days of coming ashore, following a pregnancy of eight months. To get the dates right for the annual breeding cycle they employ a process known as delayed implantation, whereby the fertilized egg only begins to grow in the womb four months after impregnation. Within five or six days of giving birth they're ready to mate again, to the final and vociferous relief of the waiting bulls.

Bulls return to the sea when their task is done, but the mothers stay at the colony, leaving for two or three days at a time to forage. Seal milk has the highest fat content of that of any mammal, and so the pups rapidly put on weight and are usually weaned within 4–6 months. During this time they molt and put on the magic coat that so nearly became the undoing of their species.

Q & A

with David Muirhead

Questions by Powers Squared Editor Matthew Powers, PhD

David, you grew up in East Africa and Great Britain and spent your adult life traveling all over the continent of Africa and living in South Africa. How did you become so interested in African wildlife? What experiences led you to writing Cat Among the Pigeons?

When I was a very small boy living in Mbale in Uganda there was a leopard in the forest abutting the bottom of our garden. The leopard and I had an understanding: I'd stay away from the bottom of the garden and the leopard wouldn't climb through my bedroom window at night. I think my dad negotiated that deal, but anyway it worked, because I'm still here today. I grew up with African wildlife, in and outside game reserves, so I was fascinated from the very beginning. I didn't get actively involved with conservation and writing about wildlife until 1999 when I founded a magazine called Wildside in partnership with KwaZulu Natal Nature Conservation, then headed up by Dr George Hughes, who was one of the world's leading authorities on sea turtles. They were also the people responsible for saving the white rhino from imminent extinction in the 1950s. I learned a lot interacting with rangers and other people working at KZN Wildlife (as it later became known) whilst researching articles in the field for the magazine, and that eventually led me to write the book.

I am like many Americans and have not had the privilege to visit Africa. But almost to a person, those lucky enough to have made the pilgrimage have an amazing story about the fauna of the continent. What do you think it is about the wildlife of Africa that sparks the imagination of Homo sapiens?

I think Africa's wild animals are, in a visceral sense, familiar to all of us, whether we've been to Africa or not. It's generally accepted that Africa was the birthplace of the human race, the nursery where we took our first baby steps as a species—the connection we feel for Africa's landscapes and wildlife is part of our DNA. That's where we grew up and they're the neighbors we interacted with. I'm often struck by the fact that children's nurseries—in the US, Europe or wherever—often feature toy elephants, lions, giraffes, hippos and the like. It's a bit fanciful, I know, but maybe not merely a coincidence that so many parents feel that their kids will be comforted by such animals, nor surprising that they are.

I have a number of graduate student friends from Africa and also American relatives and friends who have spent considerable time in Africa and they all have a story that goes something like this..."To our surprise, around the corner was a bull elephant walking toward us, flapping his ears in the middle of the mountain pass, a cliff wall on our right and a 100 foot drop on our left. Unfortunately for us, we had stripped the reverse gear out of our Land Rover earlier in the trip and...I could hear the lions sniffing and prowling outside. All I had for defense was a small pocket knife which I clutched to my chest, staring at the flimsy canvas wall of my tent...We were sitting around the low table in the middle of camp, sharing our meal with a Maasai who had wandered into camp. Suddenly, he jumped up and started beating the ground with his spear. When the dust settled, at his feet lay the corpse of the deadly...My cousin's husband's mother's best friend's child was looking for firewood one night when he was charged by a rhino. As he dodged, a boomslang landed on his head and bit him on the cheek. The sudden pain caused him to panic and he ran the wrong way, falling into the river where a hippo bit his arm off. Fortunately for him, he was able to escape before the crocodiles got the rest of him...Then, out of nowhere, a baboon..." Okay, I did make up one of these stories. So, I want to know, what is the craziest story about animals in Africa that you have heard or experienced?

One true story I'm particularly fond of involves a good friend. When she was a baby her family lived near Port Elizabeth on the east coast of South Africa. Baboons frequently raided the rural area where they lived, sorting through dustbins and sometimes barging into houses looking for food. One morning a female baboon picked up the baby (later my good friend) from a pram on the veranda. The kidnapping was witnessed by a gardener who immediately raised the alarm and gave chase. The baboon ran up a drainpipe onto the roof and sat there, alternatively examining the baby in her arms and glancing down disdainfully at the hysterical humans gathered down below. The only one who kept his cool was Grandpa. He got hold of an orange and, despite his age and creaking joints, somehow managed to get up onto the roof himself. He then negotiated with the female baboon, offering the orange in exchange for the baby. Grandpa could tell by the baboon's hesitation that it was a tough choice, but in the end she did hand over the baby and scampered away with the orange. The baby was none the worse for wear.

Every time I read Cat Among the Pigeons, *I learn something new about the animals of Africa. My favorite stories are about the more obscure animals, the more mundane. What made you include the less splashy fauna of Africa such as the coelacanth and naked mole rats?*

Most people are familiar with the big name animals—lions, elephants, etc—and I wanted to introduce the supporting cast, so to speak, the backstage characters like the aardvark. As I wrote in the book, by discarding the burrows they've dug aardvarks provide subterranean homes for a host of other creatures, and the African bush would be a very different place without them. But you could live your whole life in Africa without ever laying eyes on an aardvark. It's like that with many of the more obscure creatures, they're not high profile but they've all got a fascinating story to tell and their role in the ecosystem is often woefully underestimated or misunderstood.

I have to confess that my absolute favorite chapter in the book is about the dung beetle! I laughed and laughed but also appreciated the bug's weird and wonderful life. What was your favorite chapter to write and why?

I enjoyed writing all the stories, but some were especially challenging and fun to research. If I had to pick a favorite chapter I suppose it would be the flamingo.

I don't believe your book is about animals of Africa. I believe Cat Among the Pigeons *is about relationships. It is about the relationships of animals with each other, with their ecosystem, and ultimately humanity's relationship with our world. From your perspective, what is your assessment of the health of these relationships? Is there anything that gives you hope for the future of our planet and the animals that still exist here?*

You're right, in a very real sense the book is about relationships, what's popularly known as the web of life I suppose. Everything to do with living creatures is about the relationship, intimate or tenuous, between each individual species and the myriad others, and that includes Homo sapiens. We made a mistake about ten or twenty thousand years ago by starting to think we were the only species that really mattered. The rest were expendable dumbasses. Only now are we beginning to realize what a huge mistake that was, for them and for us.

One thing that gives me hope is knowing that around the world there are people I've never heard of doing meaningful things I may never hear about. It's easy to grow cynical and think that no one really cares what happens to African wild life but that's short changing the good guys. I'll give you one example: right now there are two rangers somewhere remote in the bush, sleeping rough, paid next to nothing, on a two month shift. I've never met them, don't know their names, but they're taking turns guarding and protecting one female rhino and her calf, following them around day and night, rain or shine. If the poachers come they'll probably be outgunned six to one, but I'm sure they'll stand their ground. Those sorts of people really care, and that's what gives me hope.

What can readers do to help protect the wildlife of Africa for future generations of humans?

The one big thing humans in general can do is restrict themselves to a maximum of two children. The explosive growth in human numbers is the single greatest threat to wild life and ecosystems in Africa, and everywhere else on the planet for that matter. There's only so much space and it's filling up too fast—with Homo sapiens and all their noxious by-products.

On an individual level, people can certainly help by giving material and vociferous support to nature conservation agencies in African countries through social media and organizations like the WWF. Conservation agencies are chronically under-resourced and beleaguered in most countries, not least thanks to their own corrupt or disinterested politicians. Yet these organizations are on the front line, their staff battling and sometimes dying to protect Africa's wildlife from poaching and rapacious human greed, often dressed up as economic development. They are fighting an insatiable monster and they need all the help they can get.

Even in Africa there is an increasing and alarming disconnect between people and wild life. As much as they're able, conservation agencies run outreach programs to educate school kids in Africa about nature and help inculcate a love for wild life and natural spaces. It's a drop in the ocean at the moment but education is key and both schools and conservation agencies could do infinitely more in this area, if they had more resources.

The book has a lot of scientific/biological info, but it's not written specifically for scientists. How do you balance the science with the art so that the book is both science-y and entertaining?

Basic zoological and biological facts are essential in understanding any animal of course, but I wanted to avoid the usual formula— height, weight, color, number of teeth, etc. Like us, animals are so much more than a list of their parts, and, like us, each one is an individual. Anyone who works with animals, or has a dog or a cat, knows that's true. But the courtesy is not usually extended to wild life and I decided to use humor, folklore, and any other bits and pieces I could get my hands on, to try and bring each creature to life in a relatable way. The aim of the book is to entertain and inform but I hope readers, scientists and lay folk alike, will come away with a more empathetic view, especially in respect of the superficially less appealing creatures.

Is there anything you would like to tell your audience about Cat Among the Pigeons *or Africa in general?*

I would urge anyone who hasn't been to Africa to make the trip at some point in their lives, if they're able to. You used the word "pilgrimage" earlier, and I think that's very revealing. If you've read the book and enjoyed it, a holiday in Africa is a chance to see some of the animals I've written about, a magical thing in itself, but at the same time it's also a way to contribute to their survival. The money tourists spend on accommodation, game drives and the like while they're visiting Africa is one of the principle factors helping ensure that the huge animal sanctuaries like Kruger and Serengeti can continue to exist.

Discussion Questions

1. Summarize the main themes in *Cat Among the Pigeons*.
   Which of those themes most connects with your life and why?
2. Which chapter was your favorite and why?
3. Why do you think David Muirhead wrote *Cat Among the Pigeons*?
   What was his purpose and does he realize his purpose in these pages?
   Who is David Muirhead writing this book for, that is, who do you
   think his intended audience is?
4. Why do you think the author included both Greek and African
   mythology in his chapters?
   What does the inclusion of both provide for the reader?
5. Do you think the author anthropomorphizes the animals in this
   book?
   Do you think it is okay to anthropomorphize animals?
   Why or why not?
   Why might scientists steer away from anthropomorphizing animals
   in their research?
6. Is this book about animals of Africa or is it about humankind?
7. Do you care more about the animals of Africa after reading this book?
   Why or why not?
8. If you were to write a chapter for the next book, what animal would
   you include and why?
9. One often quoted tenant of evolution is "survival of the fittest."
   What do you think this means?
   What does your interpretation of this statement say about the wild
   animals of the world?
10. Do you think it is important to protect ecosystems for the survival
    of wild animals?
    Why or why not?
11. Contrast the local African response to Elephants leaving game
    reserves with their response to Hippopotamuses.

What does this say about their relationship to wild animals?

12. Why do you think creatures that are not endangered were included in this book?

13. Some animals, like the rhino, are famously endangered. We know less about the dung beetle which has also been declared threatened and/or endangered in different parts of Africa.
    What is the importance of the dung beetle?
    Should we care if it's threatened or endangered?
    Why or why not?

14. What are some examples of human economics impacting animals in this book?
    How do human economic systems play into our treatment of animals?

15. Do you believe that domestic pets, such as dogs and cats, have economic value for their human companions?
    Do wild animals have economic value?

16. Do wild animals have intrinsic value?
    Why or why not?
    Can intrinsic value be quantified in monetary value?
    And should it be?

17. How much is the intrinsic value of a wild animal as an individual compared with the intrinsic value of a species?
    Is this a valid question?

18. Do you think this book is about animals or about relationships?
    If it's about animals, what is the "takeaway" message for you?
    If it's about relationships, what kind of relationships and why?

19. What is the status of the animal life in your own community?
    How can you "think globally and act locally" to influence the ecosystem positively for animals in your own community as well as for animals in places far away?

20. Looking back at the questions you've already discussed, have your answers to some of the earliest questions changed now that you've thought about the book in different ways?